Reader's Guide to the Short Story
to accompany

FICTION 100

An Anthology of Short Fiction

Eleventh Edition

James H. Pickering

University of Houston

PEARSON

Prentice
Hall

Upper Saddle River, New Jersey 07458

©2007 by PEARSON EDUCATION, INC.
Upper Saddle River, New Jersey 07458

ISBN 0-13-173391-5
Printed in the United States of America

Reader's Guide to the Short Story
to accompany

FICTION 100

An Anthology of Short Fiction

CONTENTS

PREFACE

The *Reader's Guide to the Short Story* has been prepared to accompany the eleventh edition of *Fiction 100*. It is designed to introduce readers to the fundamental elements that combine to make up a work of short fiction in order that they may be better able to analyze, understand, appreciate, and then write about what they have read. Also included here is a brief introduction to the history of the short story, so that those new to the genre can better understand the evolution and development of the short story as a distinctive and independent form of literary art. For those who would like to know more about the short story's history, a bibliography of suggested readings is provided. Once again I have included a section titled "Studying the Short Story: Additional Resources." It contains an introduction to library research, a list of resources available over the Internet, and a brief discussion and listing of adaptations of stories in *Fiction 100* which are available on video.

It is my hope that students and teachers alike will find this supplement to *Fiction 100* useful, and for that reason your reactions and comments are most certainly invited. I would especially like to thank my own students, both those at Michigan State University in years past and, more recently, those here at the University of Houston, for their contributions. My UH students, for example, made it quite clear that additional examples of "real" student writing would be helpful as they prepared to write papers on their own. I am pleased that three of those English 2305 students have agreed to allow me to include their papers in the *Reader's Guide*.

James H. Pickering
Houston, Texas

READING AND STUDYING THE SHORT STORY

Reading Critically

Whatever else they sometimes think they are, literature instructors are primarily teachers of *reading*, and their assignments are a means of involving students in a type or style of reading that is quite different from what goes on in most other courses and in the world at large. Reading literary works differs from reading most other materials mainly in the *attitude* with which we approach them. What makes our other reading seem "ordinary" is that we tend to treat it as though it carried a single message or string of information. You either "get it right" or you "misread it"—in which case the bicycle you were attempting to assemble from the "easy-to-read" instructions begins to assume strange deformities. The last thing you want from a list of mechanical instructions is "literary" ambiguity, just as the last thing you want from a mechanic (at least one acting in that capacity) is "creative" reading.

The writer of such instructions as "How to Assemble a Bicycle" tries to filter out any distracting "static" that may call attention to the language itself and distract us from the task at hand. And as readers, we try to cooperate by "editing out" any incidental "noise" (such as typos and minor grammatical errors) so as to get the information as directly and unambiguously as possible. However, the more closely we examine a work of fiction—especially when we intend to write about it—the more aware we become of all the things authors do, both intentionally and incidentally, to create diversions and booby traps as they tell their stories. What is one to make, for example, of the incident in Nathaniel Hawthorne's famous story "Young Goodman Brown" in which the traveler encountered in the woods throws his staff on the ground "where," we are told, "perhaps, it assumed life, being one of the rods which its owner had formerly lent to the Egyptian Magi"? Or the fact that the old man who Pelayo finds "moving and groaning" in the rear of his courtyard in a story by Gabriel Garcia Marquez can't get up because he is "impeded by his enormous wings"? Put simply, literary texts are more likely to *produce* questions than to answer them, and they do so in order to involve us further as active participants in the re-creation of their moods and actions.

One of the most common devices used by fiction writers to derail our determination to wring a single "message" from their stories is to incorporate

1

and affirm within their plots two powerfully held but contradictory cultural attitudes—something like: "Follow your instincts; they are the repository of your inner wisdom," and, "Resist your instincts; they are the dwelling place of your inner enemy." Such contradictions are the means by which authors give their works the feel of philosophical weight and depth and stir readers into speculation over their own values. The stress points of such conflicts, contradictions, and tensions are good places to start thinking about the theme and structure of any work of fiction. Where are the battle lines drawn? Which characters, settings, images, and attitudes belong on this side of the line and which on that? Who may be caught in the middle, torn in both directions?

Even though the pattern of conflict is fairly fundamental to the structure of all fiction, it is only one amongst an infinite variety of patterns. Language itself has meaning only because it is patterned. A certain pattern of syllables makes up a word, and a certain pattern of words makes up a statement or asks a question. When we begin to trace patterns in a literary work, any pattern—groupings of characters, the rise and fall of action in the plot, clusters of water or sun imagery—we are not simply making idle designs, but discussing *how* a work achieves its meanings.

Another word for "pattern" is "context," and virtually everything we do when we undertake to write literary criticism has to do with placing something or other—a word, a phrase, a character, a story—in its proper context. And virtually every argument between "schools" of literary criticism has to do with the question of what is or is not the "proper" context. The most immediate and available context, of course, is *the context of the work itself*. We test our feelings about a character or plot event or descriptive metaphor by placing it within or against categories developed in the same story: Is this narrator also a character in the action she is reporting? Can we entirely trust her version of this event? Has she lied to us (or to herself) elsewhere in the plot?

Most of your in-class discussions as well as the majority of your writing assignments will probably deal with individual works in isolation, but it is clear that this "isolation" is quite relative—a convenient boundary that allows one to be at least a minor expert on a particular story. The mere fact that you are writing on William Faulkner's "Barn Burning," for instance, suggests that you have an insight into the work that an ordinary or casual reader may easily have missed. And this insight may have come to you despite the fact that you haven't the slightest inkling of the rest of the fantastic "history" of the fictional Deep South country where most of Faulkner's stories and novels have their setting.

For many readers, however, "Barn Burning" hardly exists without the background of Faulkner's other fiction set in the same mythic territory of Yoknapatawpha County. The relevant context for them becomes *the context of the author's other works*. To others, it is important to know that Faulkner himself lived the greater part of his life in the town of Oxford, Mississippi, which clearly served as his model for the fictional "Jefferson." Here the context that helps to illuminate certain other features of his art is the context of the author's personal life. And none of us could read quite as much power into "Barn Burning" if we were unaware that the American Civil War, and the institution of slavery supporting a white "aristocracy," loom like ancient curses behind the action of the story. The context of social history is always present, even if we choose not to invoke it particularly, as historicist specialists might do.

Another awareness that is always present, even when we seem to be considering works in isolation, is the *context of literature itself.* To repeat a point made earlier, we are already disposed to give any writing categorized as "literary" a special kind of attention, and that kind of attention is more or less related to the status we sometimes accord writings that are, or were once considered to be, sacred or magical. There is a special excitement in the discovery that a story centering around ordinary-seeming modern events shows traces of a relationship to some of the culture's earliest forms of storytelling: folk and fairytales, myths, sagas, epics, the Bible. One does not have to listen too closely in "Barn Burning," for example, to hear echoes of Oedipus or Hamlet. As you read, try to think of other versions of the story you are reading and other variations on the same themes.

Of course, the context through which all others must be filtered is the context of the self—your own experience and values. There is no question but that your perceptions of a story are influenced by everything that you are: your sex, age, race, education, politics, religious convictions, developed likes and dislikes, and so on. And it is because of the power of this personal factor that literary papers are not simply exercises in observation, but exercises in diplomacy, as well. In certain respects, the typical paper in a literature course requires that you become almost invisible. When you are asked to write on, say, Joseph Conrad's "Heart of Darkness," you are usually not being asked for your opinion of the work. Since "Heart of Darkness" has long since been granted the status of a literary "classic," any failure on your part to appreciate Conrad's tale would most likely be regarded as a failure of imagination—your own inability to reconstruct the inherent power of the story. Actually, it may well *be* the case that your differences with the experts with respect to the quality of Conrad's fiction is simply a private matter—a question of personal taste—in which case the best you can do is to try to describe how the work is organized in some technical sense, leaving your own responses aside (for another time and place—for example, your journal, if you keep one).

But there are instances in which private issues may be public ones, as well—concerns for genuine literary debate rather than the mere wrangling over differing tastes. If you find a highly regarded literary work somehow repulsive or degrading to your own values or to human dignity in general, then you must present your case as a matter of conscience. All literary interpretation is a matter of *negotiating* a reading among all interested parties, which usually means the instructor and students of a literature class. As you have always the responsibility in your papers and comments of trying to be as sensitive as possible to the interpretive viewpoints of other readers, so should you have the right to your own informed viewpoint. In most cases instructors object to the intrusion of personal opinion into literary essays only because it is so often the mere venting of a prejudice. On the other hand, the impersonal voice can become a fetish, a pretense that someone less fallible than a human being is registering responses to the work under consideration.

Studying the Short Story

The short story as we know it today—that is, the short story as a consciously organized, highly unified piece of literary craftsmanship—is of comparatively recent origin. There have always been "stories," of course; examples of short fiction—simple, straightforward narratives in prose or verse—are to be found in the folktales, ballads, fables, myths, and legends of all nations and all cultures. At first they were circulated and passed on as part of oral tradition; later they were written down and, with the advent of printing in the fifteenth century, published and sold. Stories constitute an important part of our cultural heritage. They serve our need to share knowledge and experience, to teach, and to amuse and delight, and they have been told and written with a greater or lesser degree of sophistication depending on the maturity of the audience and, of course, the maturity of the storyteller. Such stories go by many names—tales, sketches, legends, parables, or simply anecdotes—but all provide recognizable antecedents for the modern short story. It was not, however, until less than two hundred years ago, during the early decades of the nineteenth century, that writers began to regard the short story as a literary genre all its own, whose artistic purposes, patterns, and techniques could be distinguished from all other forms of short fiction.

Like any form of art, the short story is comprised of certain identifiable devices or *elements*, each of which contributes to the making of an integrated and unified whole. When we speak of the *elements of fiction*, we are speaking of *plot, character, setting, point of view, theme, symbol, allegory, style,* and *tone.* A working knowledge of such terms is essential if we are to organize our responses to a work and to share them with others. This common vocabulary allows us to discuss literature, not just individual and isolated literary works. The elements of fiction are neither remote nor mysterious. They are the working tools of authors, critics, and intelligent readers. Their great virtue is the common ground they provide for discussing, describing, studying, and ultimately appreciating a literary work.

Plot

When we refer to the plot of a short story, we are referring to the deliberately arranged sequence of interrelated events that makes up its basic narrative structure. Most plots have an identifiable beginning, middle, and end.

In order for a plot to begin, some kind of catalyst is necessary. Some kind of existing state of equilibrium must be broken that will generate a sequence of events that taken together serve to "tell a story." Most plots originate in some kind of significant *conflict*. The conflict may be either external, when the *protagonist* (who is also often referred to as the *hero* or the *focal character*) is pitted against some object or force outside himself, or internal, in which case the issue to be resolved is one within the protagonist's own self. External conflict may take the form of a basic opposition between a man or woman and nature (as it does in Ernest Hemingway's "The Old Man and the Sea") or between an individual and society (as it does in Richard Wright's "The Man Who Was Almost a Man"). It may also take the form of an opposition between two individuals (between the protagonist and a human adversary, the antagonist), as, for example, in most detective stories, in which a Sherlock Holmes is asked to match wits with a cunning criminal. Internal conflict, on the other hand, focuses on two or more elements contesting within the protagonist's own character, as in Joseph Conrad's "Heart of Darkness," where Kurtz struggles (and fails) to subdue the savage instincts concealed beneath his civilized veneer.

Some short story plots, it should be noted, contain more than one conflict. In "Heart of Darkness," for example, while the basic conflict takes place within Kurtz, its resolution depends on Captain Marlow's determined efforts to forge his way upriver into the very heart of Africa and to rescue the man whose life and motives have become his fascination (that is, to pit himself against a hostile natural environment and the barriers imposed by the trading company's ineptness). The conflicts of a story may exist prior to the formal initiation of the plot itself, rather than be explicitly dramatized or referred to. Some conflicts, in fact, are never made explicit and must be inferred by the reader from what the characters do or say as the plot unfolds (as is the case in Ernest Hemingway's "Hills Like White Elephants"). Conflict, then, is the basic opposition, or tension, that sets the plot of a short story in motion; it engages the reader, builds the suspense or the mystery of the work, and arouses expectation for the events that are to follow.

The plot of the traditional short story is often conceived of as moving through five distinct sections or stages (a rough diagram of which follows).

1. *Exposition*: The exposition is the beginning section in which the author provides the necessary background information, sets the scene, establishes the situation, and dates the action. It usually introduces the characters and the conflict, or at least the potential for conflict.

2. *Complication:* The complication, which is sometimes referred to as the *rising action*, develops and intensifies the conflict.

3. *Crisis:* The crisis (also referred to as the *climax*) is that moment at which the plot reaches its point of greatest emotional intensity; it is the turning point of the plot, directly precipitating its resolution.

4. *Falling action:* Once the crisis, or turning point, has been reached, the tension subsides and the plot moves toward its conclusion.

5. *Resolution:* The final section of the plot is its resolution; it records the outcome of the conflict and establishes some new equilibrium. The resolution is also referred to as the *conclusion* or the *dénouement,* the latter a French word meaning "unknotting" or "untying."

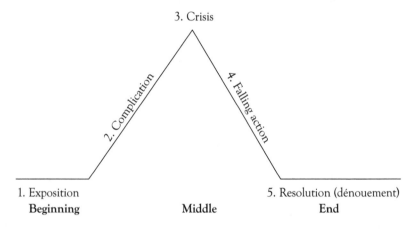

Although the terms *exposition, crisis, falling action,* and *resolution* are helpful in understanding the relationship among the parts of many kinds of narrative, not all plots lend themselves to such neat and exact formulations. Even when they do, it is not unusual for critics and readers to disagree among themselves about the precise nature of the conflict—whether, for example, the protagonist is more in conflict with society than he is with himself—or about where the crisis, or turning point, of the story actually occurs. Nor is there any special reason that the crisis should occur at or near the middle of the plot. It can, in fact, occur at any moment. In James Joyce's "Araby," and in a number of the companion stories in *Dubliners,* the crisis—in the form of a sudden illumination that Joyce called an *epiphany*—occurs at the very end of the story, and the falling action and the resolution are dispensed with almost entirely. Exposition and complication can also be omitted in favor of a plot that begins *in medias res* ("in the midst of things"). In many modern and contemporary stories the plot consists of a "slice of life" into which we enter on the eve of crisis, and the reader is left to infer beginnings and antecedents—including the precise nature of the conflict—from what he or she is subsequently able to learn.

This is the case in such stories as Ernest Hemingway's "Hills Like White Elephants" and Doris Lessing's "Wine," in which the authors choose to eliminate not only the traditional beginning, but also the ending in order to focus our attention on a more limited moment of time, the middle, which takes the form of a single, self-contained episode. Both stories offer little in the way of a traditional plot: there is limited description and almost no action. Rather, in both instances the reader overhears a continuous dialogue between two characters—a man and woman. Conflict and complication in each case are neither shown nor prepared for, but only revealed; the situation and the "story" are to be understood and completed through the active participation of the reader. Such stories are sometimes referred to as "plotless," suggesting that the author's emphasis and interest have been shifted elsewhere, most frequently to character or idea.

Selectivity

In deciding to emphasize or develop plot in a given work, how much emphasis to give individual episodes, and how these episodes are to be related to one another, the author's selectivity comes fully into play. In general, the shorter the narrative, the greater the degree of selectivity that will be required. The very economy of the short story, of course, limits the amount of plot that can be included. But no matter how much space is available, the author, in constructing his or her plot, will of necessity be forced to select those incidents that are most relevant to the story to be told. Those incidents that are the most significant will be emphasized and expanded into full-fledged dramatic scenes by using such devices as description, dialogue, and action. Other incidents will be given relatively less emphasis. In the latter case, the author may shorten the dramatic elements of the scene or eliminate them altogether in favor of summary. All these episodes, major or minor, need not advance the plot in precisely the same way or at the same pace, although the reader does have the right to expect that each will contribute in some way to the completed story.

The Ordering of Plot

The customary way of ordering the episodes or events in a plot is to present them chronologically; that is, in the order of their occurrence in time. Chronological plotting can be handled in various ways. It can be tightly controlled so that each episode logically and inevitably unfolds from the one that preceded it. It can also be loose, relaxed, and episodic, taking the form of a series of separate and largely self-contained episodes, resembling so many beads on a string. The latter is likely to be found, however, in a novel rather than a short story, simply because of the space required for its execution.

It is important to recognize that, even within plots that are mainly chronological, the temporal sequence is often deliberately broken and the chronological parts rearranged for the sake of emphasis and effect. Recall the Hemingway and Lessing stories cited above in which we encounter the characters in the middle of their "story" and must infer what has happened up to "now." In this case and others, although the main direction of the plot may be chronological and forward, the author is under no obligation to begin at the beginning. Hemingway and Lessing have us begin in the middle of things; other authors may begin at the end and then, having intrigued and captured us, work backward to the beginning and then forward again to the middle. In still other cases, the chronology of the plot may shift backward and forward in time, as, for example, in William Faulkner's "A Rose for Emily," where the author deliberately sets aside the chronological ordering of events and their cause-effect relationship in order to establish an atmosphere of unreality, build mystery and suspense, and underscore Emily Grierson's own attempt to deny the passage of time itself.

Perhaps the most frequently and conventionally used device for interrupting the flow of a chronologically ordered plot is the *flashback*, a summary or fully dramatized episode framed by the author in such a way as to make it clear that the event being discussed or dramatized took place at some earlier period of time. Flashbacks, such as young Robin's thoughts of home as he stands beside the dark church building in Hawthorne's "My Kinsman, Major Molineux," introduce us to information that would otherwise be unavailable and thus increase our knowledge and understanding of present events.

Evaluating Plot

The customary test of a plot's effectiveness is its unity: the degree to which each episode and the place it occupies in the narrative structure of the story bear in some necessary and logical (or psychological) way on the resolution of the initial conflict. In the process one can also raise questions about the plausibility of a given episode or, for that matter, about the plausibility of the plot as a whole—that is, whether the events and their resolution are guilty of violating our sense of the probable or plausible. One frequently used test of plausibility involves the author's use of *chance* (the accidental occurrence of two events that have a certain correspondence). Although chance and coincidence do occur in real life, their use in literature becomes suspect if they seem to be merely an artificial device for arranging events or imposing a resolution. Such events tend to mar or even destroy a plot's plausibility and unity.

1. What is the conflict (or conflicts) on which the plot turns? Is it external, internal, or some combination of the two?
2. What are the chief episodes or incidents that make up the plot? Is its development strictly chronological, or is the chronology rearranged in some way?
3. Compare the plot's beginning and end. What essential changes have taken place?
4. Describe the plot in terms of its exposition, complication, crisis, falling action, and resolution.
5. Is the plot unified? Do the individual episodes logically relate to one another?
6. Is the ending appropriate to and consistent with the rest of the plot?
7. Is the plot plausible? What role, if any, do chance and coincidence play?

Character

The relationship between plot and character is a vital and necessary one. Without character, there would be no plot and, hence, no story. For most readers of fiction the primary attraction lies in the characters, in the endlessly fascinating collection of men and women whose experiences and adventures in life form the basis of the plots of the stories and the novels in which they appear. Part of the fascination with the characters of fiction is that we often come to know them so well. In real life we come to know people for the most part only on the basis of externals—on the basis of what they say and what they do; the essential complexity of their inner lives can be inferred only after years of close acquaintance, if at all. Fiction, on the other hand, often provides us with direct and immediate access, however brief and fleeting, to that inner life—to the intellectual, emotional, and moral complexities of human personality that lie beneath the surface. And even when the author withholds that access, he usually provides sufficient information to allow us to make judgments about the internal makeup of the men and women to whom we are introduced. In either case, however, the ability to make such judgments—the ability to interpret correctly the evidence the author provides—is always crucial to our understanding.

When we speak of character in literary analysis, we are concerned essentially with three separate, but closely connected, activities. We are concerned, first of all, with being able to establish the personalities of the characters themselves and to identify their intellectual, emotional, and moral qualities. Second, we are concerned with the techniques an author uses to create, develop, and present characters to the reader. Third, we are concerned with whether the characters so presented are credible and convincing. In evaluating the success of characterization, the third issue is a particularly crucial one, for although plot can "carry" a work of fiction to a point, it is a rare work whose final value and importance are not somehow intimately connected with just how convincingly the author has managed to portray the characters. Naturally, such an evaluation can only take place within the context of the short story as a whole, which inevitably links character to the other elements of fiction.

The term *character* applies to any individual in a literary work. For the purpose of analysis, characters in fiction are customarily described by their relationship to plot, by the degree of development they are given by the author, and by whether or not they undergo significant character change.

The major, or central, character of the plot is the *protagonist*; his or her opponent, the character against whom the protagonist struggles or contends, is the *antagonist*. The terms *protagonist* and *antagonist* do not (unlike the terms *hero, heroine,* or *villain*) imply a judgment about moral worth. Many protagonists embody a complex mixture of both positive and negative qualities, very much in the way their real life counterparts do. The protagonist is usually easy enough to identify: he or she is the essential character without whom there would be no plot. It is the protagonist's fate (the conflict or problem being wrestled with) on which the attention of the reader is focused. Often the title of the work identifies the protagonist: "The Death of Ivan Ilych," "Young Goodman Brown," "Rip Van Winkle," "The Darling," "A Rose for Emily," and "Yellow Woman." The antagonist can be somewhat more difficult to identify, especially if he is not a human being, as is the case with the marlin that challenges the courage and endurance of the old fisherman Santiago in Ernest Hemingway's "The Old Man and the Sea." In fact, as noted above, the antagonist may not be a living creature at all, but rather the hostile social or natural environment with which the protagonist is forced to contend.

To describe the relative degree to which fictional characters are developed by their creators, critics usually distinguish between what are referred to as *flat* and *round characters.* Flat characters are those who embody or represent a single characteristic, trait, or idea, or at most a very limited number of such qualities. *Flat characters* are also referred to as *type characters,* as *one-dimensional characters,* or, when they are distorted to create humor, as *caricatures.*

Flat characters usually play a minor role in the stories in which they appear, but not always so. For example, Montresor and Fortunato are the protagonist and antagonist, respectively, in Edgar Allan Poe's "The Cask of Amontillado." Yet they are both flat characters: Montresor, who leads the unsuspecting Fortunato to be walled up in his family crypt, embodies nothing but cold-blooded revenge. And Fortunato, who appears dressed in the cap and motley of the jester, complete with bells, is quite literally a fool. Flat characters have much in common with the kind of stock characters who appear again and again in certain types of literary works (e.g., the rich uncle of domestic comedy, the hard-boiled private eye of the detective story, the female confidante of romance).

Round characters are just the opposite. They embody a number of qualities and traits, and are complex multidimensional characters of considerable intellectual and emotional depth who have the capacity to grow and change. Major characters in fiction are usually round characters, and it is with the very complexity of such characters that most of us become engrossed and fascinated. The terms *round* and *flat* do not automatically imply value judgments. Each kind of character has its uses—witness Poe's successful use of flat characters to dramatize the theme of revenge in "The Cask of Amontillado." Even when they are minor characters, as they usually are, flat characters often are convenient devices to draw out and help us to understand the personalities of characters who are more fully realized. Finally, round characters are not necessarily more alive or more convincing than flat ones. If they are, it is because the author has succeeded in making them so.

Characters in fiction can also be distinguished on the basis of whether they demonstrate the capacity to develop or change as the result of their experiences. *Dynamic characters* exhibit a capacity to change; *static characters* do not. As might be expected, the degree and rate of character change varies widely even among dynamic characters. In some stories, the development is so subtle that it may go almost unnoticed; in others, it is sufficiently drastic and profound to cause a total reorganization of the character's personality or system of values. Change in character may come slowly and incrementally over many pages, or it may take place with a dramatic suddenness that surprises and even overwhelms the character.

Static characters leave the plot as they entered it, largely untouched by the events that have taken place. Although static characters tend to be minor ones, because the author's principal focus is located elsewhere, this is not always the case. Olenka, the protagonist of Anton Chekhov's "The Darling," is a static character whose essential qualities are submissiveness and blind devotion. Without opinions, personality, or inner resources of her own, she passes through a series of relationships that leave her character essentially unchanged. But protagonists like Olenka are comparatively rare; for the most part, an author creates static characters as *foils* to emphasize, set off, and contrast the development taking place in others.

Methods of Characterization

In presenting and establishing character, an author has two basic methods or techniques at his disposal. One method is *telling*, which relies on exposition and direct commentary by the author. In *telling*, the guiding hand of the author is very much in evidence. We learn primarily from what the author explicitly calls to our attention. The other method is the indirect, dramatic method of *showing*, which involves the author's stepping aside, as it were, to allow the characters to reveal themselves directly through their dialogue and their actions. With *showing*, much of the burden of character analysis is shifted to the reader who is required to infer character on the basis of the evidence provided in the narrative. Telling and showing are not mutually exclusive, however. Neither is one method necessarily superior. Most authors employ a combination of the two, even when the exposition, as in the case of most of Hemingway's stories, is limited to several lines of descriptive detail establishing the scene.

Direct methods of revealing character—characterization by telling—include the following:

1. *Characterization through the use of names.* Names are often used to provide essential clues that aid in characterization. Some characters are given names that suggest their dominant or controlling traits, as, for example, Young Goodman Brown, the naive young Puritan in Hawthorne's story. Other characters are given names that reinforce (or sometimes are in contrast to) their physical appearance, much in the way that Ichabod Crane, the gangling schoolmaster in Washington Irving's "The Legend of Sleepy Hollow," resembles his long-legged namesake. Names can also contain literary or historical allusions that aid in characterization by means of association. One must also, of course, be alert to names used ironically that characterize through inversion. Such is the case with the foolish Fortunato of Poe's "The Cask of Amontillado," who surely must rank with the most *unfortunate* of men.

2. *Characterization through appearance.* In real life appearances are often deceiving. In the world of fiction, however, details of appearance (what a character wears and how he looks) often provide essential clues to character. Take, for example, the second paragraph of "My Kinsman, Major Molineux," in which Hawthorne introduces his protagonist to the reader. The several details of the paragraph tell us a good deal about Robin's character and basic situation. We learn that he is a "country-bred" youth nearing the end of a long journey, as his nearly empty wallet suggests. His clothes confirm that he is relatively poor. Yet Robin is clearly no runaway or rebel, for his clothes though "well worn" are "in excellent repair," and the references to his stockings and hat suggest that a loving and caring family has helped prepare him for his journey. The impression thus conveyed by the total paragraph and underscored by its final sentence describing Robin's physical appearance, is of a decent young man on the threshold of adulthood who is making his first journey into the world. The only disquieting note—a clever bit of foreshadowing—is the reference to the heavy oak cudgel that Robin has brought with him. He later will brandish it at strangers in an attempt to assert his authority and in the process reveal just how inadequately prepared he is to cope with the strange urban world in which he finds himself.

12

As in the Hawthorne story, details of dress and physical appearance should be scrutinized closely for what they may reveal about character. Details of dress may offer clues to background, occupation, economic and social status, and, perhaps, as with Robin, even a clue to the character's degree of self-respect. Details of physical appearance can help to identify a character's age and the general state of his physical and emotional health and well-being: whether the character is strong or weak, happy or sad, calm or agitated. Appearance can be used in other ways as well, particularly with minor characters who are flat and static. By common agreement, certain physical attributes have become identified over a period of time with certain kinds of inner psychological states. For example, characters who are tall and thin like Irving's Ichabod Crane and Poe's Roderick Usher are often associated with intellectual or aesthetic types who are withdrawn and introspective. Portly or fat characters, on the other hand, suggest an opposite kind of personality, one characterized by a degree of laziness, self-indulgence, and congeniality. Such convenient and economic shortcuts to characterization are perfectly permissible, of course, as long as they result in characters who are in their own way convincing.

3. *Characterization by the author.* In the most customary form of telling, the author interrupts the narrative and reveals directly, through a series of editorial comments, the nature and personality of the characters, including the thoughts and feelings that enter and pass through the characters' minds. By so doing the author asserts and retains full control over characterization. The author not only directs the reader's attention to a given character, but tells us exactly what our attitude toward that character ought to be.

By contrast, there are essentially two methods of indirect characterization by showing: characterization through dialogue (what characters say) and characterization through action (what characters do). Unlike the direct methods of characterization by telling already discussed, showing involves the gradual rather than the immediate revelation of character. Such a process requires rather than excludes the active participation of the reader by calling upon both his or her intelligence and memory.

1. *Characterization through dialogue.* Real life is quite literally filled with talk. People are forever talking about themselves and between themselves, communicating bits and pieces of information. Not all of this information is important or even particularly interesting; it tells us relatively little about the personality of the speaker, except, perhaps, whether he or she is at ease in social situations. Some light fiction reproduces dialogue as it might occur in reality, but the best authors trim everything that is inconsequential. What remains is weighty and substantial and carries with it the force of the speaker's attitudes, values, and belief. We pay attention to such talk because it may consciously or unconsciously serve to reveal his or her innermost character and personality.

The task of establishing character through dialogue is not a simple one. Some characters are careful and guarded in what they say: they speak only indirectly, and we must infer from their words what they actually mean. Others are open and candid: they tell us, or appear to tell us, exactly what is on their minds. Some characters are given to chronic exaggeration and overstatement; others to understatement and subtlety.

It is a rare work of fiction whose author does not employ dialogue in some way to reveal, establish, and reinforce character. For this reason the reader must be prepared to analyze dialogue in a number of different ways: for (1) the identity of the speaker, (2) the occasion, (3) what is being said, (4) the identity of the person or persons the speaker is addressing, (5) the quality or character of the exchange, and (6) the speaker's tone of voice, stress, dialect, and vocabulary.

In evaluating what a given character says about himself and others, one always faces (in the absence of clarifying comments by the author) the problem of the character's reliability and trustworthiness. Both deliberate deception and unconscious self-deception always lurk as distinct possibilities in fictional characters, as in real people. Although determining the reliability and veracity of characters can be difficult, most authors provide clues. When one character is contradicted in whole or part by another, the accumulated evidence on both sides must be carefully weighed and examined. One can also test reliability by looking at the character's subsequent conduct and behavior to see if what he does somehow contradicts what he says. Finally, there is always the appeal to the subsequent events of the plot itself to see whether those events tend to support or contradict the character's statements.

2. *Characterization through action.* The idea that one's behavior is a logical and even necessary extension of one's psychology and personality is widely shared. What a given character *is* is revealed by what that character *does*. In brief, the single most important and definitive method of revealing character is through action.

To establish character on the basis of action, it is necessary to scrutinize the several events of the plot for what they seem to reveal about the characters, about their unconscious emotional and psychological states, as well as about their conscious attitudes and values. Some actions, of course, are inherently more meaningful in this respect than others. A gesture or a facial expression usually carries with it less significance than some larger and overt act. But this is not always the case. Very often a small and involuntary action, by very virtue of its spontaneous and unconscious quality, tells us more about a character's inner life than a larger, premeditated act reflecting decision and choice. In either case, whether an action is large or small, conscious or unconscious, it is necessary to identify the common pattern of behavior of which each separate action is a part. One helpful way of doing so is on the basis of *motive*, the attempt to trace certain effects back to their underlying causes. If we are successful in doing so, if a consistent

14

pattern of motivation appears, then it is fairly safe to assume that we have made some important discoveries about the character.

Evaluating Character

Having identified, on the basis of the evidence presented by the author, the essential nature and personality of the characters in the work, we must also be prepared to evaluate how successful the author has been in their creation. Although it is unreasonable to expect that the characters of fiction will necessarily be close approximations of the kind of people that we know—for part of the joy of fiction is having the opportunity to meet new people—we can expect the author's creations to be convincing and credible on their own terms.

What we chiefly require in the behavior of fictional characters is *consistency*. Characterization implies a kind of unspoken contract between author and reader; and the reader has the right to expect that a character, once established, will not then behave in ways contrary to his or her nature. The principle of consistency by no means implies that characters in fiction cannot undergo development and change, for, as we have noted, the plots of many works are organized precisely on just such a possibility. Rather, when a character undergoes change, such change should be well motivated by events and consistent in some basic and identifiable way with the nature of the character. Thus, in seeking to test for consistency, we must frequently ask ourselves whether the motive for a particular action or series of actions is adequate, justified, and probable given what we know about the character.

Analyzing Character

1. Who is the protagonist of the work and who (or what) is the antagonist?
2. What is the function of the work's minor characters?
3. Identify the characters in terms of whether they are flat or round, dynamic or static.
4. What methods does the author employ to establish and reveal the characters? Are the methods primarily of showing or telling?
5. Are the actions of the characters properly motivated and consistent?
6. Are the characters of the work credible and interesting?

Setting

Fiction can be defined as character in action at a certain time and place. The first two elements of this equation, character and action, have already been discussed. Now we turn our attention to *setting*, a term that, in its broadest sense, encompasses both the physical locale that frames the *action* and the time of day or year, the climactic conditions, and the historical period during which the action takes place. At its most basic, setting helps the reader visualize the action of the work and thus adds credibility and an air of authenticity to the characters. It helps, in other words, to create and sustain the illusion of life, to provide what we call *verisimilitude*. There are, however, many different kinds of settings in fiction and they function in a variety of ways.

Some settings are relatively unimportant. They serve as little more than incidental and decorative backdrops, which have little or no necessary relationship to either the plot or the characters. Some settings, on the other hand, are intimately and necessarily connected with the meaning and unity of the total work. It is with settings of this type that as critics we must be chiefly concerned.

To understand the purpose and function of setting, the reader must pay particular attention to the descriptive passages in which the details of setting are introduced. Generally speaking, unless such passages are intended merely as local color, the greater the attention given to them, the greater their importance in the total work. In most short stories, setting is established at or near the beginning of the work as a means of orienting the reader and framing the action that is to follow. Where the emphasis on setting in such passages is slight, as it is, for example, in most of Hemingway's stories, or where the setting once established is then referred to again only incidentally, if at all, one can assume that setting as such is subordinate to the author's other concerns and purposes. If, on the other hand, the emphasis on the setting in early passages is substantial, and if similar references to the setting recur periodically as a kind of echoing refrain, one can reasonably assume that the setting is designed to serve some larger function in relation to the work as a whole.

The quality of the language by which the author projects the setting provides another clue as to his or her intention. When that intention is to invest the setting with a photographic vividness that appeals essentially to the reader's eye, the details of the setting will be rendered through language that is concrete and denotative. The author will pile specific detail on top of specific detail in an attempt to provide the illusion of a stable external reality. On the other hand, the author may want us to "feel" rather than simply "see" the setting, as is the case when setting is to be used as a means of creating atmosphere. In that case the appeal will be to the reader's imagination and emotions through language that is connotative, emotionally heightened, and suggestive. The author will, that is, manipulate the poetic qualities of language to elicit from the reader the desired and appropriate response. Often the author will want the reader to *both* see and feel the setting and will use the resources of language to bring about both effects simultaneously.

16

The Functions of Setting

Setting in fiction is called upon to perform a number of specific functions. Among them are the following.

1. *Setting as a background for action.* Everything happens somewhere. For this reason, if for no other, fiction requires a setting or background of some kind, even if it only resembles a western stage set. Sometimes this background is extensive and highly developed. In other cases, and this includes many modern stories, setting is so slight that it can be dispensed with in a single sentence or must be inferred altogether from dialogue and action. When we speak of setting as background, then, we have in mind a kind of setting that exists largely for its own sake, without necessary relationship to action or characters, or at best a relationship that is only tangential and slight.

2. *Setting as antagonist.* Often, the forces of nature function as a casual agent or antagonist, helping to establish conflict and to determine the outcome of events. The Yukon wilderness with which Jack London's nameless tenderfoot unsuccessfully tries to contend in his famous story "To Build a Fire" is an example of a setting that functions as antagonist.

3. *Setting as a means of creating appropriate atmosphere.* Many authors manipulate their settings as a means of arousing the reader's expectations and establishing an appropriate state of mind for events to come. No author is more adept in this respect than Edgar Allan Poe, who not only provides the details of setting, but tells the reader just how to respond to them.

4. *Setting as a means of revealing character.* Very often the way in which a character perceives the setting, and the way he or she reacts to it, will tell the reader more about the character and his or her state of mind than it will about the setting itself. This is particularly true of works in which the author carefully controls the point of view. In "My Kinsman, Major Molineux," for example, there is no indication that the outlandishly attired conspirators, who move easily through the streets of colonial Boston, are confused in the slightest by the city. Yet Robin, Hawthorne's young protagonist, most certainly is. For Robin the city is scarcely real; he is "almost ready to believe that a spell was on him." The dark "crooked and narrow" streets seem to lead nowhere, and the disorienting moonlight, so perfect for carrying out clandestine activities, serves only to make "the forms of distant objects" fade away "with almost ghostly indistinctness, just as his eye appeared to grasp them." The urban landscape perfectly mirrors Robin's growing sense of isolation, loneliness, frustration, and confusion.

An author can also clarify and reveal character by deliberately making setting a metaphoric or symbolic extension of character. A case in point is found in Edgar Allan Poe's "The Fall of the House of Usher." Poe begins his story with the famous passage that includes a reference to the "barely perceptible fissure" extending the full length of the house "until it became lost in the sullen waters of the tarn." As the events of the story's plot proceed to make clear, Roderick and his house are both in an advanced state of internal disintegration. Setting and character are one: the house objectifies, and in this way serves to clarify, its master.

5. *Setting as a means of reinforcing theme.* Setting can also be used as a means of reinforcing and clarifying the theme of a novel or short story. In Kate Chopin's "The Storm," the storm itself—embodying as it does the pent-up energy of nature—serves as a metaphor for the sexual passion that overcomes Alcee and Calixta. As Barbara C. Ewell notes (1986), "Chopin adroitly matches the storm's irresistible development with the effects of passion on the two . . . lovers—from the lightning bolt that occasions their first physical contact, to the convenient veil of heavy rain as they lie in bed, to their ultimate consonance with the storm's climax and gentle, exhausted retreat." The storm, in short, serves as a perfect backdrop and counterpoint for a story about repressed sexuality and sexual fulfillment outside the bonds of marriage.

Analyzing Setting

1. What is the work's setting in space and time?
2. How does the author go about establishing setting? Does the author want the reader to see *or* feel the setting; or does the author want the reader to both see *and* feel it? What details of setting does the author isolate and describe?
3. Is the setting important? If so, what is its function? Is it used to reveal, reinforce, or influence character, plot, or theme?
4. Is the setting an appropriate one?

Point of View

A story must have a plot, characters, and a setting. It must also have a storyteller: a narrative voice, real or implied, that presents the story to the reader. When we talk about narrative voice, we are talking about *point of view,* the method of narration that determines the position, or angle of vision, from which the story is told. The nature of the relationship between the narrator and the story, the teller and the tale, is always crucial to the art of fiction. It governs the reader's access to the story and determines just how much he can know at any given moment about what is taking place. So crucial is point of view that, once having been chosen, it will color and shape the way in which everything else is presented and perceived, including plot, character, and setting. Alter or change the point of view, and you alter and change the story.

The choice of point of view is the choice of who is to tell the story, who talks to the reader. It may be a narrator outside the work (*omniscient* point of view); a narrator inside the work, telling the story from a *limited omniscient* or *first-person* point of view; or apparently no one (dramatic point of view). These four basic points of view, and their variations, involve at the extreme a choice between omniscient point of view and dramatic point of view—a choice that involves, among other things, the distance that the author wishes to maintain between the reader and the story and the extent to which the author is willing to involve the reader in its interpretation. As the author moves away from omniscience along this spectrum of choices, he or she progressively surrenders the ability to see into the minds of the characters.

Commonly Used Points of View

1. *Omniscient point of view.* With the omniscient point of view, an "all-knowing" narrator firmly imposes his presence between the reader and the story and retains full and complete control over the narrative. The omniscient narrator is not a character in the story and is not involved in the plot. From a vantage point outside the story, the narrator is free to tell us much or little, to dramatize or summarize, to interpret, speculate, philosophize, moralize, or judge. He or she can tell us directly what the characters are like and why they behave as they do; record their words and conversations and dramatize their actions; or enter their minds to explore directly their innermost thoughts and feelings. The narrator can move the reader from one event to the next, being just as explicit (or evasive) as he wishes about their significance and meaning; he can skip backward and forward in time, now dramatizing, now summarizing as he chooses. When the omniscient narrator speaks to us in his own voice, there is a natural temptation to identify that voice with the author's. Sometimes such an identification is warranted; at other times it may not be, for the voice that tells the story and speaks to the reader, although it may seem to reflect the author's beliefs and values, is as much the author's creation as any of the characters.

The great advantage of the omniscient point of view is the flexibility it gives its "all-knowing" narrator, who can direct the reader's attention and control the sources of information. As we move away from omniscient telling in the direction of dramatic showing, the narrator progressively surrenders these advantages. In choosing to move inside the framework of the story to merge his or her identity with that of any one of the characters (*limited omniscient* or *first-person* point of view) or to give up all identity (*dramatic* point of view), the narrator restricts the channels through which information can be transmitted to the reader. As a result, the reader becomes more and more directly involved in the task of interpretation.

2. *Limited omniscient point of view.* With a limited omniscient (sometime referred to as *third-person*) point of view, the narrator limits his or her ability to penetrate the minds of characters by selecting a single character to act as the center of revelation. What the reader knows and sees of events is always restricted to what this focal character can know or see. This point of view differs significantly from the first-person point of view, discussed below. At times the reader may be given direct access to this focal character's own "voice" and thoughts, insofar as these are reproduced through dialogue or presented dramatically through monologue or stream of consciousness. On all other occasions, the reader's access is indirect: it is the narrator's voice, somewhere on the sidelines, that tells the story and transmits the action, characterization, description, analysis, and other informing details on which the reader's understanding and interpretation depend. Although the focal character is a visible presence within the story in a way that a fully omniscient narrator is not, that character is only as available and accessible to the reader as the narrator will permit.

The character chosen as narrative center, and often referred to through the use of a third-person pronoun as *he* or *she*, may be the protagonist or may be some other major character (for example, Charles Marlow in Conrad's "Heart of Darkness"). Often, however, the assignment is given to a minor character who functions in the role of an onlooker, watching and speculating from the periphery of the story and only minimally involved, if at all, in its action. Once chosen, it is this character's mind and eyes that become the story's angle of vision and the point of entry for the reader. Henry James aptly refers to this character in his critical essays and prefaces as "the reflector" or "mirroring consciousness," for it is through the prism of his or her conscious mind that the story is filtered and reflected.

The advantages of the limited omniscient point of view are the tightness of focus and control that it provides. These advantages explain why the limited omniscient point of view is so admirably suited to the short story, whose restricted scope can accommodate full omniscience only with great difficulty. The limited omniscient point of view is used with good effect in Hawthorne's "Young Goodman Brown," in which the author is interested in the way in which progressive disillusionment and the conviction of sin can totally influence and distort an individual's outlook. Whether or not Goodman Brown's night in the forest, climaxed by his meeting with the devil, is dream or reality finally makes no difference; Goodman Brown is convinced that "Evil is the nature of mankind." Goodman's naive and untested faith is destroyed; his vision of life is darkened; and he goes to his grave a gloomy, distrustful, and lonely man. The limited omniscient point of view serves Hawthorne's purposes well, for it is Brown's personal vision of the way that things appear to be—rather than the way that things actually are—that is at the center of Hawthorne's classic story.

3. *First-person point of view.* The use of first-person point of view places still another restriction on the voice that tells the story. As already noted, the movement from full to limited omniscience essentially involves the decision to limit the narrator's omniscience to what can be known by a single character. First-person point of view goes one step further by having that focal character address the reader directly, without an intermediary. This character refers to himself or herself as "I" in the story and addresses the reader as "you," either explicitly or by implication.

The first-person point of view thus combines the advantages and restrictions of limited omniscience with its own. As with limited omniscience, first-person narration is tightly controlled and limited in its access to information. The first-person narrator, like his limited omniscient counterpart, while free to speculate, can only report information that falls within his own first-hand knowledge of the world or what he comes to learn second-hand from others. First-person narratives are necessarily subjective. The only thoughts and feelings that first-person narrators experience directly are their own, and authors sometimes explore and exploit this subjectivity by allowing their narrators' thoughts and feelings—their perception of the world—to become colored by unwitting prejudices and biases. The implications of this uncorrected subjectivity are crucially important, for it means that the reader can never expect to see characters and events as they actually are but only as they appear to be to the mediating consciousness of the "I"-narrator who stands between the reader and the work. For this reason it is always necessary to pay particular attention to the character that fills that role—to his or her personality; built-in biases, values, and beliefs; and degree of awareness and perceptivity—in order to measure his or her reliability as a narrator.

Among the advantages of first-person point of view is the sense of immediacy, credibility, and psychological realism that autobiographical storytelling always carries with it. No other point of view, in fact, is more effective in its capacity for eliciting the reader's direct intellectual and emotional involvement in the teller and the tale.

First-person narrators are usually identified and differentiated on the basis of their degree of involvement with the events of the plot. They may be protagonists who tell stories of their own mishaps and adventures. In such works, the protagonist-narrator is always firmly in control of the content, pace, and method of presentation. Certain events will be fully or partially dramatized as the protagonist witnesses them; others will be transmitted to the reader indirectly through the use of summary and comment. Protagonist-

21

narrators, not surprisingly, tend to dominate their works to the disadvantage of other characters, and by continually calling attention to their own presence, and to their own thoughts and feelings, fully characterize themselves in the process. To the extent that such characters are perceptive and intelligent and able to make sense (and even see the irony and humor) of the events in which they participate, their stories illustrate growth and maturation. Where such sensitivity and intelligence are lacking, or where emotional clarity or even sanity are in question, as in Charlotte Perkins Gilman's "The Yellow Wall-Paper," the protagonist-narrator becomes the fit subject for irony or compassion and pity.

Protagonist-narrators may narrate events ostensibly as they take place or in leisurely retrospect, with the narrator looking backward over a period of time on adventures that have already been concluded. In retrospective views, the extent to which the narrator has managed in the interim to achieve appropriate distance and objectivity can be an issue as well. The unnamed protagonist-narrator of James Joyce's "Araby," for example, looking backward at his own adolescent romanticism, has clearly not reached such a position. In calling himself "a creature driven and derided by vanity," he is perhaps judging himself too harshly for an act that an older, and a presumably wiser, adult would be willing to excuse as part of the inevitable process of growing up.

Not all protagonist-narrators tell their own stories. Sometimes that narrator is charged with the responsibility of telling someone else's story, as, for instance, Melville's lawyer tells the story of the strange and "inscrutable" law clerk who happens into his employment and into his life in "Bartleby the Scrivener." Sometimes the first-person narrator is not the protagonist at all, but rather a character whose role in the plot is clearly secondary. He or she may, in fact, have almost no visible role in the plot and exist primarily as a convenient device for transmitting the narrative to the reader. Such is the case with Dr. Watson, the narrator of "A Scandal in Bohemia" and most of the other Sherlock Holmes stories. From his position at the periphery of the action, Watson is able to move easily among the other characters, using them as sources to acquire information. Furthermore, like other first-person narrators, Watson takes on the role of *confidant*, a genial and sympathetic personality whom Holmes treats almost as an *alter ego*, informing his clients, "This is my intimate friend and associate, Dr. Watson, before whom you can speak as freely as before myself." In a sense, however, the slow-witted Watson is also Holmes's *foil*, allowing Arthur Conan Doyle to keep his readers in the dark until the last moment about the problem solving going on in the mind of Sherlock Holmes.

First-person narrators are always subject to hidden biases and prejudices in their telling of the story. Minor characters serving as narrators, no less than major ones, must be watched constantly, especially if the reader has reason to suspect that they may be other than totally reliable guides to the truth of what they report.

4. *Dramatic point of view.* In the dramatic, or *objective,* point of view the story is told ostensibly by no one. The narrator, who to this point in the discussion has been a visible, mediating authority standing between the reader and the work, now disappears completely and the story is allowed to present itself dramatically through action and dialogue. With the disappearance of the narrator, telling is replaced by showing, and the illusion is created that the reader is a direct and immediate witness to an unfolding drama. Without a narrator to serve as mentor and guide, the reader is left largely on his or her own. There is no way of entering the minds of the characters; no evaluative comments are offered; the reader is not told directly how to respond, either intellectually or emotionally, to the events or the characters. The reader is permitted to view the work only from the outside. Although the author may supply certain descriptive details, particularly at the beginning of the work, the reader is called on to shoulder much of the responsibility for analysis and interpretation. He or she must deduce the circumstances of the action, past and present, and how and why the characters think and feel as they do on the basis of their overt behavior and conversation.

The dramatic point of view appeals to many modern and contemporary writers because of the impersonal and objective way it presents experience and because of the vivid sense of the actual that it creates. Ernest Hemingway is perhaps its leading exemplar. The dramatic mode dominates Hemingway's short stories where it is used with great effectiveness to illustrate and reinforce the psychological and emotional detachment and self-control that many of his characters adopt as a means of coping with the reality of experience.

Analyzing Point of View

1. What is the point of view: who talks to the reader? Is the point of view consistent throughout the work or does it shift in some way?
2. Where does the narrator stand in relation to the work? Where does the reader stand?
3. To what sources of knowledge or information does the point of view give the reader access? What sources of knowledge or information does it serve to conceal?
4. If the story is told from the point of view of one of the characters, is the narrator reliable? Does his or her personality, character, or intellect affect an ability to interpret the events or the other characters correctly?
5. Is the chosen point of view an appropriate and effective one?
6. How would the work be different if told from another point of view?

Theme

The *theme* is the central idea or statement about life that unifies and controls the total work. Theme is not the issue, or problem, or subject with which the work deals, but rather the comment or statement the author makes about that issue, problem, or subject.

Theme in literature is the author's way of communicating and sharing ideas, perceptions, and feelings with his readers or, as is so often the case, of probing and exploring with them the puzzling questions of human existence, most of which do not yield near, tidy, or universally acceptable answers.

Four important points about theme in fiction need to be made:

1. A theme does not exist as an intellectual abstraction that an author super-imposes on the work like icing on a cake. Rather, the theme necessarily and inevitably emerges from the interplay of the various elements of the work and is organically and necessarily related to the work's total structure and texture.

2. The theme may be less prominent and less fully developed in some works of fiction than in others. This is especially the case of detective, gothic, and adventure fiction, where the author wants primarily to entertain by producing mystification, inducing chills and nightmare, or engaging the reader in a series of exciting, fast-moving incidents. Works of this type, in fact, often do not have a demonstrable theme at all.

3. It is entirely possible that readers will differ, at times radically, on just what the theme of a given work is. Differences of opinion are perfectly accept-able as long as the interpretation being offered is plausibly rooted in the facts of the story.

4. The theme of a given work need not be in accord with the reader's particu-lar beliefs and values. We are under no obligation as readers, of course, to accept the story's theme as it is presented to us, especially if we believe that it violates the truth of our own experience and the experience of others. But we must remember that although literature is full of ideas that may strike us, at least initially, as unpleasant, controversial, or simply wrongheaded, lit-erary sophistication and plain common sense should warn us against dis-missing them out of hand. Many stories survive, in part at least, because of the fresh and challenging ideas and insights they offer. Such ideas and insights have the power to liberate our minds and our imaginations and to cause us to reflect critically about our own values, beliefs, and assumptions.

Identifying Theme

When we attempt to identify the theme of a work of fiction we are attempting to formulate in our own words the statement about life or human experience that is made by the total work. The task is often far from easy because it necessarily involves us in the analysis of a number of elements in their relation to one another and to the work as a whole. Part of the value of attempting to identify theme is that it forces us to bring together and to understand the various aspects of the work; in this process we may notice things we had previously ignored or undervalued. We will be successful in the task if we are willing to be open-minded and objective and resist the temptation to pay attention to *some* rather than *all* the elements of the work or, what is worse, to read into them what simply is not there. The identification of theme, then, is a way to test our own understandings, to focus our response, and to make the work finally and fully our own.

The ideas that constitute a work's theme may be relatively commonplace ones that easily fall within the framework of our own experience. They may also be fairly complex and abstract—somewhat hard to understand and put into words—either because we have not encountered them before or because they relate to concepts that are in themselves inherently difficult. Some themes are topical in nature (that is, they involve ideas that are valid only in relation to a specific time and place, or to a specific set of circumstances); others are universal in their application. On some occasions the theme may be explicitly stated by one of the characters (who serves as a spokesman for the author) or by the author in the guise of an omniscient narrator. Even though such explicit statements must be taken seriously into account, a degree of caution is also necessary—for characters and narrators alike can be unreliable and misleading. In many cases, however, theme is not stated but rather implied by the work's total rendering of experience; it is only gradually revealed through the treatment of character and incident and by the development of the story.

Because different kinds of works will yield different themes in different ways, there is no one correct approach to identifying theme. The following suggestions and comments, however, may prove helpful.

1. *It is important to avoid confusing a work's theme with its subject or situation.* Theme is the abstract, generalized statement or comment that the work makes about a concrete subject or situation.

2. *We must be as certain as we can that our statement of theme does the work full justice.* There is always the danger of not understanding the theme either by failing to discover its total significance or by overstating and enlarging it beyond what the elements of the story can be shown to support, and thus making the work appear more universally applicable than it is. The danger of the latter is probably greater than the danger of the former. Authors, like all intelligent people, know that universal, all-embracing statements about life are frequently refuted by the experience of individuals, and they will usually restrict their claims accordingly. They know that most of the really important questions about human experience do not yield up easy, formulistic answers. As readers, we must be careful not to credit literary works with solutions and answers where such issues and questions are only being explored or where only tentative answers are being proposed.

3. Theme was defined above as a "statement about life that unifies and controls the total work." *Therefore, the test of any theme we may propose is whether it is fully and completely supported by the work's other elements.* If our statement of the theme leaves certain elements or details unexplained, or if those elements and details fail to confirm our statements, then unless the work itself is flawed, chances are we have been only partially successful in our identification.

4. The title an author gives the work often suggests a particular focus or emphasis for the reader's attention. Just as the title of a work sometimes serves to identify the work's protagonist or essential character, it may also provide clues about theme. For example, Joseph Conrad's "Heart of Darkness" refers not only to the uncharted center of Africa, the "dark" continent, but to the capacity for evil and corruption that exists in the human heart, a title relevant to both the plot situation and the theme of Conrad's story.

Analyzing Theme

1. Does the work have a theme? Is it stated or implied?
2. What generalization(s) or statement(s) about life or human experience does the work make?
3. What elements of the work contribute most heavily to the formulation of the theme?
4. Does the theme emerge organically and naturally, or does the author seem to force the theme upon the work?
5. What is the value or significance of the work's theme? Is it topical or universal in its application?

Symbol and Allegory

Symbol

A symbol, according to *Webster's Dictionary*, is "something that stands for or suggests something else by reason of relationship, association, convention, or accidental resemblance . . . a visible sign of something invisible." Symbols, in this sense, are with us all the time, for there are few words or objects that do not evoke, at least in certain contexts, a wide range of associated meanings and feelings. For example, the word *home* (as opposed to *house*) conjures up feelings of warmth and security and personal associations of family, friends, and neighborhood, while the American flag suggests country and patriotism. Human beings, by virtue of their capacity for language and memory, are symbol-making creatures.

Most of our daily symbol-making and symbol-reading is unconscious and accidental, the inescapable product of our experience as human beings. In literature, however, symbols—in the form of words, images, objects, settings, events, and characters—are often used deliberately to suggest and reinforce meaning to provide enrichment by enlarging and clarifying the experience of the work, and to help to organize and unify the whole. William York Tyndall, a well-regarded scholar and author of *The Literary Symbol* (1955), likens the literary symbol to "a metaphor one half of which remains unstated and indefinite." The analogy is a good one. Although symbols exist first as something literal and concrete within the work itself, they also have the capacity to call to mind a range of invisible and abstract associations, both intellectual and emotional, that transcend the literal and concrete and extend their meaning. A literary symbol brings together what is material and concrete within the work (the visible half of Tyndall's metaphor) with its series of associations; by fusing them, however briefly, in the reader's imagination, new layers and dimensions of meaning, suggestiveness, and significance are added.

The identification and understanding of literary symbols requires a great deal from the reader. They demand awareness and intelligence: an ability to detect when the emphasis an author places on certain elements within the work can be legitimately said to carry those elements to larger, symbolic levels, and when the author means to imply nothing beyond what is literally stated.

Beginning readers must be particularly careful. Although the author's use of symbols may be unconscious, ours is very much an age in which the conscious and deliberate use of symbolism defines much of our literary art. There is, consequently, a tendency among students of literature, especially beginning students, to forget that all art contains a mixture of both the literal and the symbolic, and to engage in a form of indiscriminate "symbol hunting" that either unearths symbols and symbolic meanings where none are intended or pushes the interpretation of legitimate symbols beyond what is reasonable and proper. Both temptations must be avoided.

It is perfectly true, of course, that the meaning of any symbol is, by definition, indefinite and open-ended, and that a given symbol will evoke a slightly different response in different readers, no matter how discriminating. Yet there is an acceptable range of possible readings for any symbol beyond which we must not stray. We are always limited in our interpretation of symbols by the total context of the work in which they occur and by the way in which the author has established and arranged its other elements, and we are not free to impose—from the outside—our own personal and idiosyncratic meanings simply because they appeal to us. We must also be careful to avoid the danger of becoming so preoccupied with the larger significance of meaning that we forget the literal importance of the concrete thing being symbolized.

Types of Symbols

Symbols are usually classified as being *traditional* or *original*, depending on the source of the associations that provide their meaning.

Traditional symbols. Traditional symbols are those whose associations are the common property of a society or culture and are so widely recognized and accepted that they can be said to be almost universal. The symbolic associations that generally accompany the forest and the sea, the moon and the sun, night and day, the colors black, white, and red, and the seasons of the year are examples of traditional symbols. They are so much a part of our culture that we take their significance pretty much for granted. A special kind of traditional symbol is the *archetype*, a term that derives from anthropologist James C. Frazer's famous study of myth and ritual, *The Golden Bough* (1890–1915), and the depth psychology of Carl Jung. (Jung and his successors hold that certain symbols are so deeply rooted in the repeated, shared experience of our ancestors—he refers to them as the "collective consciousness" of the human race—as to evoke an immediate and strong, if unconscious, response in any reader.) Conrad's use of blackness in "Heart of Darkness," with its obvious overtones of mystery, evil, and Satanism, is an example of an archetypal symbol. Stories that focus on the initiation of the young—Nathaniel Hawthorne's "Young Goodman Brown," James Joyce's "Araby," and Katherine Anne Porter's "The Grave"—all carry with them archetypal overtones. Frazer discovered that such rites of passage exist everywhere in the cultural patterns of the past and continue to exert a powerful influence on the patterns of our own behavior.

Original symbols. Original symbols are those whose associations are neither immediate nor traditional; instead, they derive their meaning, largely if not exclusively, from the context of the work in which they are used. Perhaps the most famous example of an original symbol is Herman Melville's white whale, Moby Dick. Whereas whales are often associated in the popular imagination with brute strength and cunning, Moby Dick assumes his larger, metaphysical significance (for Captain Ahab, he is the pasteboard mask behind which lurks all the pent-up malignity of the universe) only within the contextual limits of Melville's novel. Outside that novel, a whale is just a whale.

Use of Symbols

Setting and symbol. In a number of the examples used in the discussion of setting—the storm that brings Kate Chopin's characters Alcee and Calixta together, Roderick Usher's ancestral mansion, and the city streets through which Robin roams in search of his kinsman—we noted how the details of setting are used functionally to extend and clarify the author's larger intention and meaning. We also noted the fact that authors frequently call attention to the seasons of the year and the time of day because of the traditional associations these have for the reader. These identifications are not arbitrary ones, for in each of the works cited, the author deliberately calls attention to the setting, not once but on several occasions, in a way to suggest that it is integrally related to his or her larger purposes. In the case of Chopin, it is to call attention to the thematic implications of the work; in the case of Poe and Hawthorne, it is to help establish the personalities of their characters. Setting in fiction that goes beyond mere backdrop is often used in such symbolic ways. Symbolic settings are particularly useful to authors when they frame and encompass the events of plot and thus provide the work as a whole with an overaching pattern of unity.

Plot and symbol. Single events, large and small, or plots in their entirety often function symbolically. Even the most commonplace action or event—even to the level of gesture—can carry symbolic meaning, though it is often difficult, at least upon first reading, to tell for certain whether symbolism is involved. The symbolic nature of plot or plot elements may not, in fact, become clear until after we have finished the work and look backward to see how the individual parts of the plot relate to the whole. In Hawthorne's "My Kinsman, Major Molineux," for example, it may not be clear until the end of the story that each of the separate incidents that punctuate Robin's journey in search of his kinsman form a chain of symbolic events that are an integral part of his ritual of initiation.

When the entire sequence of events that constitute a plot falls into a symbolic pattern as in "My Kinsman, Major Molineux," the events are often archetypal. Such a plot, that is, conforms to basic patterns of human behavior so deeply rooted in our experience that they recur ritualistically, time and time again, in the events of myth, folklore, and narrative literature. In fiction, perhaps the most frequently encountered archetypal pattern is the journey or *quest,* in which young men and women undergo a series of trials and ordeals that finally confirms their coming of age and newfound maturity.

Character and symbol. Symbolism is frequently employed as a way of deepening our understanding of character. Some characters are given symbolic names to suggest underlying moral, intellectual, or emotional qualities. The name "Robin," for example, suggests springtime, youth, and innocence. The objects assigned to characters function in the same way: the heavy oak cudgel that Robin carries with him into the city functions as a symbol to suggest his youthful aggressiveness; Miranda's attention to the carved wedding ring that her brother has discovered in the grave in Katherine Anne Porter's "The Grave" symbolizes her vague intimations of the role in life she is destined to play; the gun that Dave covets in Richard Wright's "The Man Who Was Almost a Man" is the symbol of the masculine independence that is not yet his; and the house in which Emily Grierson has lived so long in William Faulkner's "A Rose for Emily" functions as an analogy to Emily herself, "lifting its stubborn and coquettish decay" alone and apart.

Although the personalities of major characters are often revealed and clarified through the use of symbols rooted in the language that describes them, their very complexity as human beings usually prevents their being defined by a single symbol. This is not true of minor characters, especially those who are flat and one-dimensional and are constructed around a single idea or quality. Literature is filled with such individuals. The girl in James Joyce's "Araby," significantly known only as "Mangan's sister," in whose service and religious-like adoration the narrator visits the bazaar, symbolizes the mystery, enchantment, and "otherness" that typifies a young boy's first love. In Conrad's "Heart of Darkness," the Director of Companies, the Lawyer, and Accountant who sit on the deck of the *Nellie* in the "brooding gloom" of evening listening to Marlow recount his journey in search of Kurtz symbolize the type of men who are incapable of appreciating or understanding the moral complexity of experience. Self-satisfied, complacent men, who have become successful by mastering the practical affairs of the world, are "too dull even to know (that they, too) are being assaulted by the powers of darkness."

Symbolism thus enhances fiction through helping readers to organize and enlarge their experience of the work. This is not to say that a work of fiction containing symbolism is inherently or necessarily better than one that does not. Nor is it to say that symbolism in and of itself can make a given work successful. It is to say that symbolism, when employed as an integral and organic part of the language and structure of a work of fiction, can stimulate and release the imagination—which is, after all, one of the major goals of any form of art.

Allegory

Allegory is a technique for expanding the meaning of a literary work by having the characters, and sometimes the setting and the events, represent certain abstract ideas, qualities, or concepts—usually moral, religious, or political in nature. Unlike symbolism, the abstractions of allegory are within the context of a particular tradition, fixed and definite, and likely to take the form of simple and specific ideas that, once identified, can be readily understood. Because they remain constant, they are also easily remembered. In their purest form, works of allegory operate consistently and simultaneously at two separate but parallel levels of meaning: one located inside the work itself, at the concrete level of plot and character; the other, outside the work, at the level of the particular ideas or qualities to which these internal elements point. Such works function best when these two levels reinforce and complement each other: we read the work as narrative, but are also aware of the ideas that lie beyond the concrete representations.

The most famous sustained allegory in the English language is John Bunyan's *The Pilgrim's Progress* (published in two parts, in 1678 and 1684). In Bunyan's book, the didactic impulse always latent within allegory is very clear. *Pilgrim's Progress* is a moral and religious allegory of the Christian soul in search of salvation. It tells the story of an individual, appropriately named "Christian," who sets off in search of the Celestial City (heaven) and along the way is forced to confront obstacles whose names and personalities (or characteristics) represent the ideals, virtues, and vices for which they stand within Bunyan's Christian tradition: Mr. Worldly Wiseman, Mistrust, Timorous, Faithful, Giant Despair, the Slough of Despond, the Valley of the Shadow of Death, and so on.

Although works of pure allegory like Bunyan's are relatively rare, many works do make occasional use of allegory, not infrequently combined with symbolism. As a fictional mode of presentation, however, allegory is unquestionably out of favor among modern and contemporary authors and critics, for reasons that have to do with the nature of allegory itself. First of all, the didacticism of allegory and its tendency toward a simplified, if not simplistic, view of life is suspect in a world where there is very little common agreement about truth and the validity of certain once universally respected ideas and ideals. Second, the way allegory presents character is simply not in keeping with the modern conception of fictional characterization. In allegory the characters, and the ideas and ideals those characters embody, are presented as a given. The modern author, on the other hand, prefers to build characters and to develop and reveal their personalities gradually, in stages, throughout the course of the work.

Several of the stories included in *Fiction 100* either contain clear instances of the use of allegory or lend themselves to allegorical readings. The name Faith, which Hawthorne gives to the wife of Young Goodman Brown, is certainly, in part at least, intended allegorically. "With Heaven above, and Faith below, I will yet stand firm against the devil!" Goodman Brown cries out as he approaches his midnight rendezvous, and in the pages that follow, his exhortations to "Faith" clearly refer not only to his wife, whom he fears is numbered among the devil's communion, but to his Puritan religious faith that is itself being tested. An allegorical reading has also been suggested for Hawthorne's "My Kinsman, Major Molineux." Read as a historical and political allegory of America's coming of age and maturation as a young and independent nation, Robin can be said to represent Colonial America and his kinsman the traditional British authority that must be displaced and overthrown. Both Robin and colonial America share a number of common characteristics: both have rural, agrarian origins; both are young and strong, yet insecure and self-conscious because untested and inexperienced in the ways of the world; both are pious and proud (even arrogant) and given to aggressive behavior; and both have a reputation, deserved or not, for native "shrewdness." Just as Robin learns that he can "rise in the world without the help of [his] . . . kinsman, Major Molineux," so colonial America realizes that it can achieve its destiny as a mature and independent nation without the paternalistic control of Great Britain. In each of the preceding examples, an allegorical interpretation does seem to "work," in the sense that it allows us to organize the elements of the story around a central illuminating idea. Nevertheless, it would be a mistake to press such readings too far. To read these works exclusively as allegories is to oversimplify the internal dynamics of each story and to distort the author's vision.

Analyzing Symbol and Allegory

1. What symbols or patterns of symbolism (or allegory) are present in the story? Are the symbols traditional or original?
2. What aspects of the work (e.g., theme, setting, plot, characterization) does the symbolism (allegory) serve to explain, clarify, or reinforce?
3. Does the author's use of symbolism (allegory) seem contrived or forced in any way, or does it arise naturally out of the interplay of the story's major elements?

Style and Tone

Style

The distinctive quality of literature that sets it apart from all other forms of artistic expression is its reliance on language. Using words is the writer's craft. Words are the writer's means of recovering and objectifying experience; and they are his or her means of presenting, shaping, and controlling subject matter. Language is also the means by which the writer controls and influences the reader: in responding to literature we are always responding to and through the author's words. The literary critic must pay close attention to those words; not only because they convey the sum and substance of the author's message—the story he or she wishes to tell—but because they provide important clues to the author's emotional and psychological life, beliefs, and attitudes and the way in which he or she perceives and experiences the self and the world.

When we talk about an author's words and the characteristic way he or she uses the resources of language to achieve certain effects, we are talking about style. In its most general sense, style consists of *diction* (the individual words an author chooses) and *syntax* (the arrangement of those words and phrases, clauses, and sentences), as well as such devices as rhythm and sound, allusion, ambiguity, irony, paradox, and figurative language.

Each writer's style is unique. It constitutes his or her "signature" in a way that sets the work apart. One test of the distinctiveness of the author's style is its ability to resist paraphrase. The test is relatively simple. Take a passage from any well-regarded work and paraphrase it. Although the underlying ideas may remain the same, the words themselves will probably register a quite different effect on you.

By examining the style of a work of fiction we are seeking as critics to accommodate a number of objectives. First of all, we are seeking to isolate and identify those distinctive traits that comprise the author's "signature." Second, we are interested in understanding the effects produced by particular stylistic devices and techniques and how these effects influence our response to the work's other elements—particularly character, incident, setting, and theme—and to the work as a whole. Third, we are attempting, by way of evaluation, to arrive at a judgment based on a consideration of just how effectively the author has managed to integrate form and content. This examination is an attempt to measure just how well an author has succeeded in a given work with the style he or she has chosen.

Elements of Style

The following are some basic elements of style that we examine to characterize an author's writing.

Diction. Although words are usually meaningful only in the context of other words, stylistic analysis begins with the attempt to identify and understand the type and quality of the individual words that comprise an author's basic vocabulary. When used in connection with characterization, words are the vehicles by which a character's ideas, attitudes, and values are expressed. Words convey the details of outer appearance and inner state of mind. In dialogue they reflect the speaker's level of intelligence and sophistication, general level of conscious awareness, and socioeconomic, geographical, and educational background. When used to describe incidents, words help to convey the narrator's (or author's) attitude toward those events and the characters involved in them. When used to describe setting, words help to create and sustain an appropriate atmosphere.

The analysis of diction includes the following considerations: the *denotative* (or dictionary) meaning of words, as opposed to their *connotative* meaning (the ideas associated or suggested by them); their degree of *concreteness* or *abstractness*; their degree of *allusiveness*; the *parts of speech* they represent; their *length* and *construction*; the *level of usage* they reflect (standard or nonstandard; formal, informal, or colloquial); the *imagery* (details of sensory experience) they contain; the *figurative devices* (simile, metaphor, personification) they embody; their *rhythm* and *sound patterns* (alliteration, assonance, consonance, onomatopoeia). In studying diction, we also need to pay close attention to the use of *repetition*: the recurrence of key words in a given passage or series of passages in such a way as to call special attention to themselves.

Syntax. When we examine style at the level of syntax, we are attempting to analyze the ways the author arranges words into phrases, clauses, and finally whole sentences to achieve particular effects. Although syntax is determined partly by the lexical content (or meaning) of the words and partly by the basic grammatical structure of the language, every writer enjoys considerable freedom to shape and control the syntactic elements of style. In looking at an author's syntax we want to know how the words have been arranged and particularly how they deviate from the normal and expected.

Although one can study syntactic units smaller than the sentence—for example, individual phrases that call attention to themselves by their length, content, and placement—syntax is probably most easily approached and analyzed in sentences. Such an approach mirrors most closely the writing process itself, for sentences are the major units of thought, and it is on the crafting of sentences that most authors concentrate their creative energies. Sentences can be examined in terms of their length—whether they are short, spare, and economical or long and involved; in terms of their form—whether they are simple, compound, or complex; and in terms of their construction—whether they are loose (sentences that follow the normal subject-verb-object pattern, stating their main idea near the beginning in the form of an independent clause), *periodic* (sentences that deliberately withhold or suspend the completion of the main idea until the end of the sentence), or *balanced* (sentences in which two similar or antithetical ideas are balanced).

Each type of sentence will have a slightly different effect on the reader. Long, complicated sentences slow down and retard the pace of a narrative, whereas short, simple sentences hasten it. Loose sentences, because they follow the normal, predictable patterns of speech, tend to appear more natural and less contrived than either periodic or balanced sentences, particularly when they are used in the creation of dialogue. Moreover, the deliberate arrangement of words within individual sentences or groups of sentences can result in patterns of rhythm and sound (pleasant or unpleasant) that establish or reinforce feeling and emotion. Although an author will usually vary the kinds of sentences used to avoid monotony (unless monotony is intended), certain syntactic patterns will dominate and become characteristic of that author's style.

34

Style can be used as an aid to characterization, the creation of setting and atmosphere, and as a means of reinforcing theme. Stylistic comparisons between authors provide instructive lessons in the dynamic, changing nature of the language itself. Comparing the style of Edgar Allan Poe to the style of Ernest Hemingway, for example, allows us to appreciate the movement in fiction toward less formality and more concrete diction, as well as simpler syntax, reflecting the modern tendency toward realism in fiction. Comparative generalizations about style, however, can be dangerous. Style is a highly personal and sometimes a highly idiosyncratic matter, open to endless opportunities for innovation and experimentation. Although some fictional styles are easier to read and understand than others, and although all readers sooner or later come to express stylistic preferences, there is, finally, no one style that is best or most appropriate. The critic's job is to try to understand the distinctive elements that comprise an author's style, the various effects that those elements create, and the way in which they serve to reveal and reinforce the other elements of the work.

Tone

All of us are familiar with the term *tone* as it is used to characterize the special qualities of accent, inflection, and duration in a speaker's voice. From early childhood on we learn to identify and respond to these elements of speech. For example, a mother can tell her child to "Come here" in a manner that is angry, threatening, concerned, amused, sympathetic, or affectionate, simply by altering her tone of voice. In each case, the mother's meaning is the same—she wants her child to come to her. However, the relationship she creates with her auditor (the child) will differ dramatically according to her tone. Tone, then, is a means of creating a relationship or conveying an attitude. The particular qualities of a speaking voice are unavailable to a writer in creating tone, but to a certain extent rhythm and punctuation can substitute for a speaker's accent and inflection; word order and word choice can influence tone as easily in prose as in speech.

Just as the tone of the mother's voice communicates her attitude of anger or concern, so tone in fiction is frequently a guide to an author's attitude toward the subject or audience and to his or her intention and meaning. As critics we infer the author's tone through close and careful study of the various elements within the work, including plot, character, setting, point of view, and style. No matter how hard an author tries to mask his or her attitudes and feelings, and to hide his or her presence within the work, perhaps by taking refuge somewhere behind the narrative voice that tells the story, the author's tone can be inferred by the choices he or she makes in the process of ordering and presenting the material—by what is included and emphasized and what, by contrast, is omitted.

The literary critic learns to look at such choices carefully—at the characters, incidents, setting, and details depicted; at the issues and problems that are raised and explored; at the style the author has employed; at every decision, in short, that the author has made—to infer from them the underlying attitudes and tone that color and control the work as a whole.

Irony. When the young girl in Sandra Cisneros's "The House on Mango Street" addresses us, she is frank and open, and though she may not fully appreciate the implications of her story, there is little reason to believe that she means anything other than what she says. The same thing, however, is not always true of Sandra Cisneros herself, who is on most occasions likely to be circumspect and cautious and prefer to adopt a posture of detachment and objectivity. Authors like Cisneros know all too well that life is not always simple and straightforward; that the affairs of men and women, young or old, are full of surprises, ambiguities, contradictions, and complexities; and that appearances can and often do deceive. To reflect the puzzling, problematic nature of experience, such authors choose to approach their subjects indirectly, through the use of irony. They use techniques to create within a work two separate and contrasting levels of experience and a disparity of understanding between them.

The three types of irony that occur most frequently in literature are *verbal irony* (in which there is a contrast between what a speaker literally says and what he or she means), *irony of situation* (in which an event or situation turns out to be the reverse of what is expected or appropriate), and *dramatic irony* (in which the state of affairs known to the reader or the audience is the reverse of what its participants suppose it to be).

Verbal irony is easily recognized in speech because of the intonation of the speaker's voice. For example, when Mark Anthony refers to Brutus in Shakespeare's *Julius Caesar* as "an honorable man," few members of the audience are likely to misunderstand the irony in his statement. When used in fiction, however, verbal irony is sometimes more difficult to identify because it is conveyed exclusively through the author's style, through the words on the printed page. Sometimes the author helps the reader by means of repetition, as Hawthorne does in "My Kinsman, Major Molineux," where Robin, the uninitiated youth from the country, prides himself on his native "shrewdness." Shrewd, at least in the way of the city, Robin is most certainly not.

Irony of situation, on the other hand, results from the careful manipulation of plot, point of view, setting, and atmosphere. Robin's prolonged and frustrating search for his kinsman, for example, is rendered ironic by the fact that his arrival in Boston coincides exactly with a revolutionary plot whose chief object is the very individual who Robin believes will help him rise in the world. Robin is but one in a long line of fictional characters whose expectations are altered or reversed by the events that overtake them. The situational irony in Hawthorne's story is sustained not only by the plot, but by the point of view, which reveals the true state of things only gradually both to Robin and to the reader. In Shirley Jackson's "The Lottery," irony of situation is established by the ostensibly gay and lighthearted atmosphere and festive scene on the June morning on which the story opens, and by Jackson's use of a detached and matter-of-fact dramatic point of view. Only as the events of the morning unfold does the reader come to grasp the underlying horror of ritualistic violence that the villagers are about to perpetrate on one of their own.

Dramatic irony, like irony of situation, depends on the use of plot, character, and point of view. An omniscient narrator, for example, will sometimes reveal information to the reader that his characters do not know; this allows the narrator (and the reader) to judge the subsequent actions of those characters and to anticipate the likely outcome of events. Dramatic irony can also be established by means of characters whose innocence and naiveté cause them to misperceive or misinterpret events whose significance is perfectly clear to the reader. The plots of such works frequently turn on the matter of knowing or not knowing, and result in outcomes that are either comic or tragic in their final implication.

As critics Robert Scholes and Robert Kellogg note in their study of narrative literature, *The Nature of Narrative* (1966), there are "In any example of narrative art . . . broadly speaking, three points of view—those of the characters, the narrator, and the audience." When any of the three "perceives more—or less—than another, irony must be either actually or potentially present." In any work of fiction, it is crucially important that we are able to determine if and how that potential has been exploited; to overlook or misinterpret the presence of irony can only lead to a misinterpretation of the author's attitudes and tone and the way he would have us approach and understand the work.

Analyzing Style and Tone

1. Describe the author's diction. Is the language concrete or abstract, formal or informal, literal or figurative? What parts of speech occur most often?
2. What use does the author make of imagery; figurative devices (simile, metaphor, personification); patterns of rhythm and sound (alliteration, assonance, consonance, onomatopoeia); repetition; allusion?
3. Are the sentences predominantly long or short; simple, compound, or complex; loose, periodic, or balanced?
4. Describe the author's tone. Is it, for example, sympathetic, detached, condescending, serious, humorous, or ironic? How is the tone established and revealed?
5. What kind(s) of irony does the author use: verbal irony, irony of situation, dramatic irony? What purpose(s) does the irony serve?
6. What are the distinctive characteristics of the author's style? In what ways is the style appropriate to the work's subject and theme?

37

WRITING ABOUT THE SHORT STORY

Reading and Writing

Contrary to rumor, literary criticism is not always an exercise in human ingenuity that professors of English engage in for its own sake or to impress one another. Neither is the word *criticism* to be confused with the kind of petty fault-finding we sometimes encounter in caustic book reviews. Literary criticism is nothing more or less than an attempt to clarify, explain, and evaluate our experience with a given literary work. It allows us to explain what we see in a literary work that others may have missed or have seen less clearly. It allows us to raise and then answer, however tentatively, certain basic questions about an author's achievement and about the ways in which he or she achieved it. It also allows us to form some judgments about the relative merit or quality of the work as a whole. Literary criticism is a method of learning about literature, and the more we learn about how to approach a story, poem, or play, the greater our appreciation of a truly great work becomes, and greater still the sense of pleasure and enjoyment we can derive from it.

Literary criticism is the inevitable by-product of the reading process itself, for if we take that experience seriously, then criticism of some sort becomes inevitable. The only question is whether the judgments we form will be sensible ones. Literary criticism begins the moment we close our book and start to reflect on what we have just read. At that moment, to be sure, we have a choice. If we have been engaged in light reading, say a detective story, where our interest and curiosity are satisfied once the solution to the crime is revealed and the criminal apprehended, we may simply put the book aside without a second thought and turn to other matters. Such an act, in itself, is a judgment. But if our reading has moved us intellectually or emotionally, we may find ourselves pausing to explore or explain our responses. If, in turn, we choose to organize and define those responses and communicate them to someone else—to a parent, a roommate, or close friend—we have in that moment become a literary critic.

For many of us this kind of engagement is most likely to take the form of written essays on subjects assigned to us or of our own devising. Writing about literature, in this case the short story, is in fact the logical, even necessary, extension of the process of analysis discussed above. Writing critically about what we have read provides us with the opportunity and occasion to extend the kind of relationship with a given work in a way that makes that work finally and fully our own. Like all writing activities, writing about literature also helps us to develop and improve our skills of interpretation and expression in a way that will serve us well in a wide variety of other intellectual activities. Thinking critically about literature is not easy. Neither is writing about literature. Both are acts of exploration and discovery. Both require the trial and error that attends any new learning activity and the patience to persevere until the process itself becomes comfortable.

For those of you who are already experienced at writing about literature and have long since developed your own methods and approaches, some of the following discussion may seem too elementary or too obvious. On the other hand, teachers of literature are notorious for assuming that when they ask for a five-page paper (due next Tuesday) on "something in *The Red Badge of Courage* that interests you," you automatically know how to go about producing whatever it is they expect. For those of you who are relatively new at the task, or even those of you who would like to rethink your strategies for writing about fiction, this segment of the *Reader's Guide* tries to place in plain view some of the general assumptions instructors have in mind when they ask you to write about literature. Please remember, however, that these are only general recommendations, and any specific requirements of an assignment must naturally be given priority.

In addition, because most instructors of literature courses tend to take composition skills for granted, you may be interested in some of the suggestions made here from recent composition theory about more effective ways to generate ideas for papers as well as ways to take some of the anxiety out of the writing process. A final section provides a brief guide to some of the *formal* requirements of the literary essay, from the format of the brief undocumented paper through the first steps of the research paper. For less common examples of quotation and documentation you should consult the *MLA Handbook for Writers of Research Papers*, 6th ed. (New York: Modern Language Association of America 2003).

Even for good readers, however, getting ideas on paper can be sheer agony, and in many cases, it is those writers who set the highest standards for themselves who anguish most over their writing. The causality is circular: writing is painful because it is done with such a sense of judgmental pressure; the next time you are asked to do any writing, your tendency will be to put it off until the last moment, and thus you find yourself again having to perform under the worst possible circumstances: trying to get everything right on the first draft, editing and polishing as you go, relying on pure association for the organization of your thoughts. All this while trying at the same time to guess which approach is most likely to appeal to this particular instructor.

Anyone who has ever attended college has had to rely from time to time on the night-before-due method of paper writing. Writing is a very personal activity, and in many instances, the best advice is to stay with what has worked best for you in the past. But anyone, no matter how experienced in writing, can get stuck staring at a blank page or word-processor screen for whatever reason.

The following discussion is based on the best *general* advice developed by modern composition theory for generating ideas about a topic and keeping them fluid until (but not before) they are developed fully enough to consider polishing for presentation to an audience. You may wish to eliminate or change the order of some of the recommended steps to fit your personal style, but the principle of constructing most of the paper *prior to any thought toward an audience* is a sound one and should be seriously considered.

1. The First Reading

I have already discussed the reading of the work you plan to write about to some extent. Whether you have a previously assigned topic or are free to choose your own, keep in mind as you read that the "casual" reader is one who makes ready and easy assumptions, filling in the gaps and filtering out the annoying inconsistencies, trying to make "ordinary" sense out of an extraordinary text. However, the quality of your attention should be quite different from that of a casual reader. You do not assume things so easily or take the "world" of the fiction for granted. On the contrary, you will want to ask yourself what and how much the reader must grant to make that world possible. "Do people *really* talk like that?" How have we been led by the author to think that they might? How is the style of dialogue related to the story's setting? Through whose eyes are we seeing the action? Do those eyes see everything, even what other people are thinking? Read with a pen or pencil in hand and mark up your text (if you own it) or take notes on any feature of the story that you feel may have been overlooked by your hypothetical "casual reader." Do not assume that any such observations are necessarily "deep." Sometimes the most obvious features of a story are ignored precisely because they *are* obvious, rather like the envelope in Poe's "The Purloined Letter."

2. Freewriting

After having read and considered the story you are planning to write about, it is often very helpful to put yourself through a stint (or several stints) of nonstop, freely associative writing. In this kind of writing you should not concern yourself with logic or style or punctuation or any other standard of correctness. The whole point of this exercise is to get down as many impressions of the work you have just read without having to consider any particular use for what you are writing. Try to keep in mind through *all* of these first stages of composition that if you find yourself stuck or spending long periods hovering over one sentence or paragraph, it is probably because you are prematurely considering an audience and feeling judged for what you are attempting to put on paper. The following is one student's thoughts on Faulkner's "Barn Burning":

The Snopses seem mean and stupid. Especially the daughters seem stupid I dont know about the rest of them, the mother seems nice. I dont know why sarty is going to tell on his father. Why hes different than his father and more like his mother who wants to help him after the fight. But for some reason the father knows Sarty wants to tell on him but I dont know why. The mansion owner is right to try to make Pap clean the rug but I wouldnt have taken it to their house to get it cleaned. The father is so touchy that he will try to do something mean to anybody who tries to get back at him, but he always moves away to another place, so when he gets to Despains mansion he walks right in and ruins the rug. He makes very racist remarks But so does the man in the first lawsuit. On the night of the fire Sarty gets away and runs to the mansion to tell on his father and then he runs away into the forest.

3. Listing Ideas and Questions

It is impossible to tell in advance what your freewriting might produce, but *anything* is better than a blank page. Go through what you have and underline whatever looks to you like a possible idea or a significant question. There are no rules for this. All you are trying to do at this point is to lift fairly solid material from the irrelevant verbiage. Make a loose list of the items you have culled and arrange them in any order that seems logical to you. Here is the same student's list of remarks and questions derived from her freewriting.

1. Are the Snopses stupid? The brother and two sisters are. The mother and the aunt just seem afraid. Pap is just mean and will do anything to get back at someone.

2. Sarty is more like his mother.

3. Why does Sarty want to tell and how does his father know that he does?

4. The father does mean things but nobody can get back at him because they can't prove any thing.

5. Pap tracks manure on the expensive rug on purpose.

6. All the people in the story seem kind of racist.

7. Sarty and his mother know what Pap is going to do when he gets the oil cans.

8. Why does Sarty try so hard to tell on his father?

4. The Thesis Sentence

After reviewing the list of ideas and questions you have drawn from your freewriting, you should have a relatively clear notion of the concerns of the story that most attract your attention. Try to formulate in a full sentence, with complete subject and predicate, the point that you plan to explore or demonstrate in your paper. "Faulkner's attitude toward the Old South in 'Barn Burning'" is a topic, but "Faulkner's attitude toward the Old South in 'Barn Burning' is revealed by the ambiguity of the story's ending" is a *thesis statement*. Go back to your freewriting sessions if no central idea has formed itself solidly enough yet for you to produce a satisfactory thesis sentence. Eventually the tendency of your writing will help you discover the points of doubt in your reading of the story that you feel are in need of exploration and clarification. The student writing on "Barn Burning" found that she could not write a thesis statement without first condensing her list of ideas:

1. The father does mean things to other people and they can't do anything about it because he has nothing to lose.

2. No matter how hard he tries, Sarty is more like his mother than like his father.

3. Why does Sarty want to tell on his father?

She was then able to formulate her thesis sentence:

Sarty wants to tell on his father because he is more like his mother and doesn't want to be a "lone wolf" like his father all his life.

44

5. Rereading the Text

Once you have stated the thesis of your paper, it will probably be necessary for you to go back to the text of the story to find and note supporting evidence for your point of view. Don't be afraid to alter your thesis if you find that the facts are other than how you remember them. The implications of the story will keep growing for you throughout your involvement with it. If you are planning a more formal study with references to the opinions of others, you should now have a firm enough sense of direction to begin your research. The time-honored system for keeping track of notes and the books and journals from which the notes are taken is to keep two sets of index cards (usually 3 x 5s and 5 x 8s), one set with full bibliographical information on each of the sources, and the other set with the notes keyed by number or letter to the source from which each was taken. The method may seem very fussy, but anyone who has ever painstakingly copied out quotations for a paper and was later unable to identify their source because of a failure to make an adequate bibliographical entry will appreciate the need. If there is even a remote chance that you may cite a work, make up a card on it. You never know what turns of argument your paper may take to bring you back to it.

6. The Rough Draft

Once you are satisfied with your thesis statement and feel that you have enough specific illustration for it from the text (and from whatever secondary sources you may have consulted), you are ready to try a rough draft. Once more, it is important to keep in mind that you are still writing for yourself, and writing as much to discover and explore ideas as to express them. Use as your organizing principle for this first full version of the paper the same list that you made after freewriting, with whatever additions and revisions your survey of the evidence has suggested. Once you have a sense of the major divisions of your argument, you should write fairly rapidly without fussing over style or grammar or spelling. What you should be aiming for at this point is mainly to "fill up" each section of the rough draft with as many associated ideas as possible. Cutting surplus material later on will always be easier than trying to eke out an anemic, under-developed section of the essay. Don't bother to copy quotations into this draft. Either number the location of each quotation as it occurs to you while writing, or go back after you have finished writing and note the strategic location for each reference. If you have taken notes on cards, you will now be able to arrange them in the order they will most likely be used in the later drafts.

Here is the rough draft of the paper on "Barn Burning" we have been following:

Pap Snopes is a mean man who always thinks he has to get even with somebody for one thing or another. He is like a lone wolf who doesn't care for anything and during the civil war he stole horses from both the North and the South. He was shot in the foot getting away with one. He is a sharecropper and hardly owns any thing. So he can always do something to people who own farms and they cant fight back because he hasnt got any thing that they can take from him. He doesnt even seem to love his family much because he's always yelling at them or hitting them like when he hits because he say Sarty would of told the truth.* Even though the story doesnt tell why Pap thinks so. He is like a flat tin figure because he doesn't feel anything.* He only cares for getting even, and thats what he has been doing all his life. The family has had to move from one place to another constantly because of Pap burning down barns. When the story starts there is a trial about the barn of a man named Harris that burned down. He made Pap pay a dollar to get a pig back that kept getting loose and going into Harrises yard. Sarty has to think very hard about what enemies these people are because he <u>thinks</u> he is on his father's side. When they ask Sarty to stand up and testify he becomes very frightened and confused.

Sarty is really more like his mother than he is his father, even though he keeps trying to think and act like his father. He gets in a fight with a bigger boy when the other boy calls him a barn burner. When he starts to get into the wagon his mother feels sorry for him and wants to wash the blood and dirt off his face but Pap wont allow it. Also the mother has kept a pearl-inlaid clock that she had from before she was married. Even though the clock no longer works.* She doesnt have any other pretty thing in her own life, but she is very much against her husband's destruction of other peoples property like the de Spain's rug.

When Sarty goes with his father to see their new landlord he is very impressed with the mansion. He believes that people who live in a house like this are out of reach of his father and that is father

will finally have some respect for property. But
this is just when his father decides to walk through
some fresh manure. Pap pushes the de Spain's black
butler out of the way and tracks the manure right
onto an expensive rug in the hallway. When he leaves
he turns on his foot and grinds the dirt farther
into the carpet. Out side he tells Sarty that this
big house was built with "nigger sweat," meaning
slavery, and that "white sweat" is supposed to make
it even bigger.* Pap is not going to let anyone richer
than he is push him around. But that is why he is
always getting even and having to move.

When major de Spain brings the rug for Pap to clean,
pap goes out to the field and gets a sharp stone for
his daughters to scrub it with. They also use strong
lye on it. The major is going to make Pap pay for it
with twenty bushels of corn from the fall harvest,
but Pap sues de Spain instead. When the trial comes
up Pap is only made to give five dollars worth of
corn for a hundred dollar rug, but he still is not
satisfied and decides to burn down de Spain's barn

to get even with him. The mother tries to stop him but he won't listen. Sarty tries at first to believe that he is true to his father, but something makes him break away to warn the de Spains. He has turned away from his father because he wants to believe that people who have beautiful things are more like his mother than his father. They are more civilized. But we still have to think of the way the de Spains made their money, and we are not sure whether Pap was so much worse than they are.

7. The First Revision

Ideally you will have begun writing early enough to allow you time to put the rough draft away for a few days so that you may approach it again with a fresh eye and some objectivity. The reason you have been urged to produce so much loose, baggy writing in the first two stages of the paper is so that at this stage, the first revision, your problem will not be production but weeding and cutting. By now you should have an abundance of good ideas and they should be in a relatively logical order. The point is to accomplish most of the *creative* work of the paper on your own terms without having to consider a reader.

Now, in your first revision, the major task is to turn private writing into public communication. In most instances, your real and final audience is your instructor, the person who will be assigning grades. If you find it useful in your work of revising the rough draft to think of pitching your tone and style directly to that audience, then by all means do so. But many student writers find it more helpful to think of their peers as the audience of their writing. This does not mean simply people of your own age or scholastic level, but the members of your present literature class, who, even though they may not be much like you in background or even age, share in common the influence of the ideas of one another and of the same instructor. In other words, your class constitutes a community of readers, and when you think of them as an audience, you should also have in mind the agreements and disagreements that are current within the group. Another technique that some writers find helpful in establishing an appropriate tone and style for their argument is to imagine a "casual reader" who is not inattentive or insensitive, but understandably eager to brush aside irritating complications to the story's "ordinary" sense. Your rationale as "a more careful reader" is to point out that the story is not really following the paths we are accustomed to taking in our less attentive readings, and then to trace the resulting implications of this more tangled track.

However, to talk about such things as tone is to get somewhat ahead of ourselves. The first concern in revising with a reader in mind is to get your material into its most effective and logical order. What this means in plain terms is placing your generalizations in some close relationship with the particular evidence you plan to use in support of them. Short papers can be organized in a simple *particular to general* pattern (usually the close *explication* or glossing of a brief section of the text followed by a discussion of the implications of this section for the rest of the story), or from the *general to the particular* (comments on some larger element of the fiction, such as character or setting, illustrated by quotations from relevant points in the text). But your audience should never be left wondering for very long "Why am I being asked to read all these quotations (or all this plot summary)?" or "What makes this person think *this* is so?" Some appropriate conclusion should be fairly close at hand following the citation of textual evidence, and any claim to a special understanding of the text or to knowledge of obscure facts of history requires a reasonably handy reference to some source for the idea or information. In this phase of your writing you should cut mercilessly any unsupported assertions and any excess, functionless quotations or plot summaries.

8. The Final Draft

Perhaps the single most important determining factor in the success or failure of your literary essay is the skill you show in moving between the level of generality and the level of specific detail. This is why you are urged to take such care with the arrangement of assertions and their support in the first revision of your paper. In the final draft the main concern is with the transitions between those larger building blocks of your paper: how you introduce arguments and their supporting evidence, and how you follow up on them once they have been introduced. It is largely a matter of finding the best "voice" to suit the kind of material under discussion. As a general principle you should take care to be as sensitive as possible to the mood of the literary moments you are presenting. Worse than not quoting at all is to quote and then make some cute, anticlimactic comment that shatters the dignity of a passage (or bluntly misses its humor). It is not a bad idea to get a friend to listen to your paper read aloud. Someone who knows you should be able to tell whether you are sounding like yourself or putting on some pompous or coy vocal disguise. Your arguments may be cogent enough, but you still must convince any reader that you are an honest and competent guide to the work under discussion.

Following is the final draft of the student paper on Faulkner's "Barn Burning." It is by no means perfect, but it tries quite successfully to explain the motivation of the boy, "Sarty" (whose actual name is Colonel Sartoris Snopes). One of its real victories is that it catches the irony of the fact that the boy who wants so badly to belong somewhere ends up running away from his own family.

Odd Son Out

The character of Pap Snopes in William Faulkner's story "Barn Burning" is somewhat like that of a lone wolf. He has courage and cunning and is unafraid of people who have power and money because he doesn't have anything to lose and they do. He seems to have no love for anyone or anything, and Faulkner describes him as always looking the same in his black coat, like "something cut ruthlessly from tin" (40). The one thing that does matter to him is getting even, and he does that with barn burning. The family has had to move more than a dozen times in the last ten years.

The Story starts out with a trial in a country store where Pap is accused of having burned the barn of a man named Harris. They have no solid proof, but Harris wants Pap's youngest son, Sarty, to testify. Sarty has been sitting there saying over and over to himself that these people are his enemies, but he is very confused when they want him to tell the truth. Throughout the story he constantly tells himself that he feels the same way about things as his father does, but Pap somehow knows he is different. After the trial he takes Sarty aside and says, "You were fixing to tell them. You would have told him" (39) and then hits the boy.

Sarty's mother is not at all like Pap, or like her twin daughters of elder son either. when Sarty gets hurt in a fight with a much bigger boy who calls him a "barn burner," the mother feels sorry for him and wants to wash the blood and dirt off his face, but Pap won't allow it. When they leave that place and finally reach the next house they are going to live in, the mother and aunt begin unloading furniture while the two huge, "bovine" daughters just sit in the wagon until Pap orders them out. In the load with the furniture is a "clock, inlaid with mother-of-pearl which would not run, stopped at some fourteen minutes past two o'clock of a dead and forgotten day and time, which had been his mother's dowry" (37). The clock seems to be the only pretty thing in the mother's life and it is broken. It is all she has left of the home she had before she met Abner Snopes.

The only child in the family at all like the mother is Sarty. When Pap takes him along to meet their new landlord, Sarty is very impressed with the mansion where the de Spains live: "<u>Hit's as big as a courthouse</u> he thought quietly" (40). He believes that people who live in such a place can't be touched by his father. They are too far above him. But that's just when Pap decides to push his way in past the black butler, tracking fresh horse manure in on an expensive rug and grinding it in further as he turns on his heel to leave. Outside they stop for a moment to look back at the big house and Pap says, "'Pretty and white, ain't it? That's sweat. Nigger sweat. Maybe it ain't white enough yet to suit him. maybe he wants to mix some white sweat with it'" (41). We now know that Major de Spain has made his fortune with slaves. Pap is never going to allow the wealthy to push him around, but that is why he is always getting even and having to move, too.

Pap purposely ruins the rug Major de Spain brings for him to clean, and it is the lawsuit over the rug that leads Pap to another barn-burning party. Sarty's mother begs her husband not to do it, just as she begged him not to ruin the rug, but she is afraid to try and stop him. Sarty tries as usual to believe he will stick with his father, but his father knows better, and he's right. The story ends with Sarty being the cause of his own father's death and running away like a "lone wolf" himself. The reasons for his actions are never very clear in the story, but he seems to want most to belong somewhere. Perhaps he believes that people who care for pretty things are kind and sympathetic like his mother. But then again we have to remember how the de Spains got what they have.

9. The Finished Paper

In your final draft, questions of style are largely taken care of by the way in which you imagine yourself moving from point to point—as a teacher, as a guide, as a passionate advocate, as a somewhat removed skeptic—whatever you find the appropriate role for this particular exercise. But you also have to attend to all the fundamentals of composition from sentence structure to spelling before typing the copy that you plan to submit to your instructor.

Finally, as a last step, carefully *proofread* your paper and ink in whatever minor corrections that may be necessary. In format, the finished paper should be typed and double-spaced (or the handwritten equivalent if allowed), with one-inch margins on all four sides—about 250 words per page.

Quotation and Documentation

In most brief papers, your quotations will be taken from a single story and from an edition of that story used by the entire class as a text, in which case full bibliographical citation is not really necessary. It should be obvious from your introductory paragraph which work you are about to discuss. Place direct quotes within quotation marks and include the page reference, set in parenthesis outside the quotation marks but within the closing punctuation of the sentence, to help your reader locate the passage in question.

"After the kings of Great Britain had assumed the right of appointing the colonial governors," states the narrator of Nathaniel Hawthorne's "My Kinsman, Major Molineux, "the measures of the latter seldom met with the ready and general approbation which had been paid to those of their predecessors, under the original charters" (47).

Notice that the language of the quotation is woven into the sentence structure of the paper so as not to be too disruptive of the flow of the discussion.

To keep the verb tense scheme simplified, literary discussions are generally conducted in the "literary present" tense, as if the action of the plot were a *continuing* one (the character "says," the character "does," the character "goes,"), even though stories are most often narrated in the *past* tense. Sometimes it becomes necessary to change the grammar of the quoted material to make it fit into the context of your own discussion. Any such alterations of the original (or additions, as when vague pronoun references must be identified) are indicated by the use of square brackets.

Miss Spencer's friend notes that "He [the cousin]

wore a slouched hat and a rusty black velvet jacket,

such as I had often encountered in the Rue

Bonaparte" (726).

For most general discussions of a work, it is wise to keep the number and length of direct quotations to a minimum. However, in those cases in which you find yourself having to quote more than four lines of uninterrupted prose, the conventional way to set off such passages is to single-space and double-indent. Quotation marks (except for those already present in the source) are unnecessary because the format already marks off the inserted material from your own writing.

> Julian raised his eyes to heaven. "Yes, you
> should have bought it," he said. "Put it on
> and let's go." It was a hideous hat. A purple
> velvet flap came down on one side of it and
> stood up on the other; the rest of it was green
> and looked like a cushion with the stuffing
> out. He decided it was less comical than jaunty
> and pathetic. Everything that gave her pleasure
> was small and depressed him. (455)

Note that the parenthetical page reference is still used, but in this case with two spaces *following* the closing punctuation of the final sentence.

When you begin quoting sources from outside your course text, you will have to provide your reader with the information needed to locate the passages in question. If you are writing about a single story, the title and author of which are clear from the context of your discussion, again, as with your course-text references, you must place the page number(s) in parentheses at the end of the quotation. But it is also necessary to identify, either at the foot of the page or at the end of your paper, the precise edition of the work to which your page numbers refer. For example:

Charles Peacock, from V. S. Pritchett's "The Fall,"

reminds me in certain ways of Woody Allen,

especially in the way that "crowds and occasions"

frighten both of them, and engage them in "the

fundamental battle of . . . life: the struggle

against nakedness, the panic of grabbing for clothes

and becoming someone" (81).[1]

---

[1]All quotations of "The Fall" are from *V. S. Pritchette: Selected Stories*. 1978. New York: Vintage, 1979.

The rules for quoting from fiction are quite simple: either your quotations are direct (in which case you must indicate so with the proper punctuation and page reference) or they are not. If you are not quoting directly, you may paraphrase or summarize a story as much as you like without providing a page reference for every allusion to the plot. However, when you begin to incorporate materials from critical and scholarly texts into your papers, the rules are much more strict. Certainly you must continue to indicate in the usual ways any direct reproduction of the language of your source,

One introduction to <u>The Red Badge of Courage</u> points

out that publication of the novel "made Crane a

famous man" (Crews ix).

but along with the acknowledgements of direct quotations from critical and scholarly works, you must also give fair credit for any material that you *paraphrase* or *summarize*. The original language of a passage from Ludwig Lewisohn's *The Story of American Literature* (New York: Random House, 1939) runs as follows:

> Within nine years after the publication of "A Chance Acquaintance" Howells had not only made himself master of his craft and method but reached his highest point of power. The intervening novels, especially "The Undiscovered Country," which deals sanely and finely with spiritualism and "Dr. Breen's Practice," a spirited defense, within his limitations of course, of the professional woman, have in an increasing degree both his virtues and his graces as a novelist. (248)

A summary of Lewisohn's passage might read

> Not many years after having written "A Chance
>
> Acquaintance" Howells had hit the stride of his style
>
> with such novels as The Undiscovered Country
>
> and Dr. Breen's Practice (Lewisohn 248).

Even if you completely rephrase the observation in your own language, you have not come to this judgment of the progress of William Dean Howell's art independently, but have chosen to use even Lewisohn's example titles for the framing of the time scheme. Thus, you owe him an acknowledgment either by way of the parenthetical reference, or better yet, simply by beginning the above summary with "As Ludwig Lewisohn points out . . ." or other similar introductory phrase. The failure to do so constitutes plagiarism just as much as if you had directly copied the passage, or even its key words or phrases.

If you really *need* another writer's key words and phrases for the sense of your own argument, then go ahead, help yourself. Just make sure that there is always a clear boundary between your own and the other person's language, such as:

> Lewisohn claims that "within nine years" after "A
>
> Chance Acquaintance" was published, Howells had
>
> reached the "highest point of his power" as a novelist
>
> with such books as The Undiscovered Country and
>
> Dr. Breen's Practice (248).

or even

> Howells's Dr. Breen's Practice has been called a
>
> limited but "spirited defense" of the right of women
>
> to enter into the professions (Lewisohn 248).

If you will look again at the above examples of scholarly citation you will notice that the author's names are mentioned in the body of the paper or are included with the parenthetical page references. If you should happen to be citing *two* works by the same author in your paper, enough of each title should be included as well to make it distinguishable from the others when your reader turns to your list of Works Cited (discussed in more detail below). A reference to Chester Anderson's article, "The Sacrificial Butter," might be placed at the end of a quotation or paraphrase in your essay as,

(Anderson "Butter" 52–53)

while a citation of his book *Word Index to Stephen Hero*, could be shortened to

(Anderson <u>Index</u> 98)

Finally, all parenthetical references must be fully identified in a list of Works Cited, alphabetically arranged according to the authors' last names, on a separate page at the end of your paper. There your reader should be able to find all the information needed to locate the sources to which your parenthetical notations refer. Following are the formats for some of the most common kinds of entries in a list of Works Cited:

A Book by a Single Author

Parker, Hershel. <u>Herman Melville: A Biography,</u>

<u>1819–1851</u>. Baltimore: Johns Hopkins University

Press, 1996.

1. Author's name
2. Title of the book
3. Place of publication, name of publisher, date of publication

A Book by Two Authors

Pickering, James H., and Jeffrey D. Hoeper. <u>Concise</u>

<u>Companion to Literature</u>. New York: Macmillan, 1981.

1. Author's name

2. Title of the book
3. Place of publication, name of publisher, date of publication

A Book by Three or More Authors

Baugh, Albert C., et al. <u>A Literary History of England</u>.

New York: Appleton, 1948.

1. First Author's name followed by the abbreviation "et al." ("and others")
2. Title of the book
3. Place of publication, name of publisher, date of publication

An Introduction, Preface, or Foreword

Pickering, James H. Editor's Introduction. <u>The Parks</u>

<u>and Mountains of Colorado. A Summer Vacation in</u>

<u>the Switzerland of America, 1868</u>. By Samuel

Bowles. Norman: U of Oklahoma P, 1991.

1. Editor's/Author's name
2. Title of part of book
3. Title of book
4. Author of book
5. Place of publication, name of publisher, date of publication

A Work in an Anthology

Conrad, Joseph. "The Secret Sharer." <u>Literature</u>. 5th

ed. Ed. James H. Pickering and Jeffrey D. Hoeper.

Upper Saddle River: Prentice Hall, 1996.

1. Author's name
2. Title of work
3. Title of anthology
4. Edition of anthology
5. Editor(s)'s name(s)
6. Place of publication, name of publisher, date of publication

A Translation

Tolstoy, Leo. <u>War and Peace</u>. Trans. Louise and Alymer

Maude. New York: Simon and Schuster, 1942.

1. Author's name
2. Title of work
3. Translator(s)'s name(s)
4. Place of publication, name of publisher, date of publication

An Article in a Scholarly Journal

Powell, Jon. "The Stories of Raymond Carver: The

Menace of Perpetual Uncertainty." <u>Studies in the</u>

<u>Short Story</u> 31 (1994): 647–656.

1. Author's name
2. Title of article
3. Title of scholarly journal
4. Volume number
5. Issue number if needed (for journals that page issues separately)
6. Date of publication
7. Page number(s)

A Review

Lodge, David. Rev. of <u>Guided Tours of Hell: Novellas</u>.

By Francine Prose. <u>New York Times Book Review</u>

12 January 1997: 7.

1. Reviewer's name
2. Title of work being reviewed
3. Author of work being reviewed
4. Title of series (journal, newspaper, etc.) containing review
5. Date of review
6. Page number(s)

Publication Accessed from a CD-ROM

<u>The Oxford English Dictionary</u>. 2nd ed. CD-ROM.

Oxford, Eng.: Oxford UP, 1992.

1. Name of author (if given)
2. Title of work being reviewed
3. Edition, release, or version (if relevant)
4. Publication medium (CD-ROM)
5. Place of publication, name publisher, date of publication

(If not all the information is available, cite what is.)

Material Accessed through a Computer Service

Mikosh, Bert A. "A View of 'Young Goodman Brown.'"

Online. Internet. 15 Jan. 1997.

1. Name of author (if given)
2. Publication information for printed source (including date, if given)
3. Title of data base (if given)
4. Publication medium (Online)
5. Name of computer service
6. Date of access

(If not all the information is available, cite what is.)

An Electronic Text

Poe, Edgar Allan. "The Cask of Amontillado." <u>Unabridged</u>

<u>Edgar Allan Poe</u>. Philadelphia: Running Press, 1983.

Online. U of Virginia Lib. Internet. 15 Jan. 1997.

1. Name of author (if given)
2. Title of text
3. Title of work (if given)
4. Place of publication, name of publisher, date of publication
5. Publication medium (Online)
6. Name of repository of electronic text
7. Name of computer network
8. Date of access

(If not all the information is available, cite what is.)

Footnotes or Endnotes

Of course, traditional footnotes or endnotes numbered sequentially through the paper are still acceptable, and even preferred by some writers, because the system allows them to take the reader aside for incidental commentary, and to end their sentences cleanly without parenthetical references dangling off the end. As its name suggests, the footnote is placed at the foot of the page on which its reference number occurs,[1] is single-spaced, and appears four spaces below the text.[2]

----

[1]Eugene Current-Garcia, <u>The American Short Story Before 1850</u> (Boston: Twayne, 1985) 112.

[2]As you are probably aware, considerable debate goes on over the question of when the short story as a true genre actually began.

Endnotes (as one would expect) are placed on a separate page at the end of the paper, but are double-spaced. Both endnotes and footnotes have their *first lines* indented, in reverse fashion from items in the list of Works Cited.

A third alternative is to use parenthetical page references and a list of

Works Cited for source documentation, *along with* foot or endnotes. The numbered notes may serve either for extensions of the discussion too awkward to include in the main text, or for evaluative comments on sources that may or may not appear in the Works Cited list. Again, for more extensive examples see the MLA *Handbook for Writers of Research Papers*, 6th edition.

Points to Remember

1. *Critical writing, like all writing, involves five stages of the writing process: prewriting, writing, revision, editing, and proofreading.* It also takes time. Be certain that your own writing schedule allows adequate time for each. This is particularly true of prewriting (the time you set aside to study the text, brainstorm, and plan your essay) and revision (the time you set aside to rethink and rewrite what you have already written).

2. *As part of the prewriting stage, make sure that you fully understand just what is expected of you*—including your instructor's protocols governing length, format, and deadlines—as well as the standards against which your completed essay will be evaluated. If the topic or thesis has been assigned in advance by your instructor, your options are limited, and your task, in some respects, at least, is easier. If the assignment is more general, you must be extremely careful that the topic or thesis you choose is of manageable size and, of course, that it is worthy of study in the first place. If your essay takes the form of an analysis that focuses on one or more of the elements of fiction, you would do well to review the questions posed at the end of each section of the discussion above.

3. *Before you begin to write, be sure to reread the text as many times as necessary to make absolutely certain that you understand exactly what is there*—no more and no less. Proceed by taking notes, marking individual lines or passages, and making marginal notations to use later on as the source of ideas or evidence when you begin to organize and write your essay. The more times you reread the text, the most likely you are to understand it.

4. *Buy a good dictionary, and refer to it as often as necessary.* Many words have changed their meanings (sometimes dramatically) over time, and the correct *denotative* meanings of a particular word must be understood before any attempt is made to construct an analysis or argument around its *connotations*.

5. *In writing an analysis, it is essential that you supply sufficient evidence from the text to support your reading of it.* Individual words, phrases, lines, and passages should be properly quoted. Quote directly when necessary, unless the passage quoted would be so long as to be obtrusive. Be sure to enclose the quoted materials in quotation marks. You can and should be selective here, using ellipses to indicate omission. (Ellipses are three periods—evenly spaced—or a fourth period where your omission includes the end of the sentence.)

6. *Don't summarize.* Analysis is dependent upon interpretation, not summary. Some summary is, of course, necessary as a means of orienting the reader and organizing your ideas. But summary alone (simply rehashing what happens or what is said in the story) is not an adequate substitute for a discussion of what makes the work effective or important. An exception is the review, a type of writing about literature not yet touched upon. Reviews, of the sort that commonly appear in newspapers and magazines, are usually intended for audiences who are not familiar with the work being discussed. Here some summary statements about what the work is all about, together with comments about the author and his or her other works, are highly appropriate and, in the case in which the work being discussed is a new one, probably necessary in order to orient the reader. In short, in reviews summary statements will tend to occupy far more space than would be appropriate in an analysis, where the reader's general familiarity with the work can be assumed.

7. *Organize your ideas.* In writing an analysis the method of organization is one of the key decisions that must be made as you plan your paper. The question of how to organize an analysis is usually most easily resolved by allowing the major ideas marshaled in support of your thesis to become the controlling subjects of your individual paragraphs.

8. *Use the library when appropriate.* College and university libraries are filled with books and periodicals that provide analyses of literary works, and the question of whether or not they should be consulted in approaching your own writing assignment is one that inevitably arises for most students. Your instructor is the best authority here, for he or she can tell you not only whether or not such research is expected or appropriate, but if it is, just where you may most profitably begin. A brief introduction to such resources follows below.

Remember always that published critics are simply intelligent readers who have practiced the art; they are never to be regarded as the final authority about a given work, though some tend to write with a degree of positiveness that might lead you to think otherwise. Remember, too, that if you do consult such sources and make use of ideas that are not your own, your indebtedness must be fully and appropriately acknowledged through citations of the sort that have been discussed above.

9. *Don't be afraid to ask for help.* Writing effective papers on literary subjects is a developed skill. It takes time, and it takes effort. But if you are spending both and still not getting the results you want, by all means seek out your instructor and ask for his or her advice. Schedule an appointment during your instructor's office hours, and then come prepared, bringing with you what you have already written for the course, so that your meeting will be as productive as possible. You should also be sure that you know what additional resources your school makes available to students, including whether or not it has a writing center where you can obtain additional help with your writing problems. It should go without saying, but most instructors genuinely appreciate students who seem to care about their education.

Three Sample Student Essays

Reprinted below are three papers written by students taking English 2305 (Introduction to Fiction) at the University of Houston in response to the following assignment: Write a 1,000 word essay on the characters in a story of your choice. These are not, I hasten to add, first drafts. The students were given the opportunity to revise their papers making use of the comments and suggestions that I had earlier offered. In almost every other respect, however, they are "unvarnished": they appear here as they were handed to me (I do confess to having made a few silent corrections for the sake of appearance). I am grateful to all three writers for giving me their written permission to use their work as illustrations for this guide. The authors hope, as I do, that they will prove helpful to others embarking on the challenging adventure of writing about literature.

As you read these essays, note the following:

1. The student-authors have provided good topic paragraphs in which they identify story and author and make it clear to the reader what to expect in the body of the paper. In this respect the essays on Anton Chekhov's "The Darling" and Tobias Wolff's "Powder" are the more traditional. Both these papers begin by appealing to the experience of the reader. "In the course of our lives," the author of the Chekhov paper notes, "we have all met a woman who has not developed thoughts, feelings, or even her own sense of well being." The author of the Wolff paper begins: "Life is about taking risks."

The author of the Chekhov paper then introduces Olenka as an example of such a woman and then observes that her "behavior raises the question about how a woman like Olenka functions with others and why would anyone call her 'The Darling.'" Her topic paragraph concludes with a succinct statement of purpose: "An analysis of her character will answer this question."

The author of the paper on Tobias Wolff's "Powder" offers by way of introduction not one but two general statements, and then in sentence three directly links them to the theme of the story. He next tells the reader that the

66

work presents in father and son "two fundamentally different personalities" and that the Wolff makes "extensive use of symbols and figurative language" to develop in the reader "a deeper sense of the two conflicting characters." As in the case of the first paper, by the time we have finished the topic paragraph we have a good idea what to expect in the paragraphs that follow.

The author of the essay on Irwin Shaw's "The Girls in Their Summer Dresses" uses her topic paragraph to do much the same thing. She clearly establishes the central problem or issue with which the story deals—in this case, the complex and conflicted attitudes that Michael and Frances bring to their marital relationship—and tells us that her essay will examine "the complex emotional relationship of this pair."

All three authors, in short, have heeded my oft-repeated injunction: to be effective a paper must have a clear and focused topic paragraph. When writers fail to provide one—when they fail to establish at the outset what they are up to and why—more than likely trouble looms ahead!

2. The organizational pattern of each essay follows naturally from its topic paragraph. None of the authors are slavishly dependent on retelling ("rehashing") the facts of the plot. They assume that the reader is familiar with the story at hand. In making her argument, the author of the essay on "The Darling" sensibly (and briefly) traces the history of Olenka's successive relationships with the males who come into her life as a way of illustrating her blind devotion. While this author is intent on identifying and explaining the factors which reveal Olenka's behavior, and organizes her paper accordingly, the author of the Shaw essay is dealing with a single relationship—with two characters not one. She appropriately organizes her essay by discussing Michael's character (he is of course the focal character) and then turns to the character of Michael's wife, Frances.

By contrast, the author of the essay on "Powder," having announced his interest in exploring the ways in which symbol and language serve to reveal character, focuses the body of his paper on specific episodes and events, anchoring his discussion on the given facts of the story and the language used by the characters in talking about them.

3. All three essays offer ample evidence for the assertions and statements they make by making excellent use of the details of the text. Quotations are appropriately referenced with page numbers, so that the reader may return to the original text if necessary to view the context from which they are taken.

4. The essays end as well as they began—and most importantly they do so without simply repeating their opening paragraphs (a temptation which should be avoided). The author of the essay on "The Darling" does repeat the question she had posed in her opening paragraph as a way of reminding the reader of

the problem she has been addressing. Her conclusion is contained in the final two paragraphs, which do a nice job of summarizing what she has discovered about Olenka. In the last sentence the author offers a final judgment about this unfortunate woman. Though there is always a danger that such judgments are rooted in the writer's own beliefs and prejudices, and not the details of the story, that is not the case here. The judgment offered seems fully justified by what the author has told us in the preceding paragraphs.

In the final paragraph of her essay on "The Girls in Their Summer Dresses," the author does a nice job of summarizing exactly where Irwin Shaw has left his "ill-starred" lovers. As her analysis has shown, "Their opposing feelings about the components of a successful marriage have driven a wedge between the two. . . ."

The essay on "Powder" has a similarly effective ending. Having used the preceding paragraphs to explore the differences between father and son, the author uses his final paragraph to explore briefly the "shared insight" which the two have reached, coming to rest on the narrator's (the son's) final, and penultimate, statement, "If you haven't driven fresh powder, you haven't driven."

5. Let me reiterate what I said earlier: these are not first drafts. While in each case the original essay showed promise, all three required revision to give them the level of polish and sophistication they now demonstrate. The authors heeded the advice given earlier: that good papers, like good wine, require a measure of aging and incubation. They need to sit so that when we return to them we do so with a measure of freshness and objectivity. In addition, the revision process always requires an expenditure of time and effort, a willingness to review with an open mind the comments and suggestions previously received (from instructor or friendly reader), and a willingness to rethink and rework much of what has been previously written. In a word, good papers are the product of hard work. Astonishingly enough, the grade given to the first draft of the essay on Tobias Wolff's "Powder" was a C-.

6. Finally, and most importantly, however different they are in subject and approach, these three essays, in their final state, share three further attributes that every professor values highly: they are well written; they are cleanly edited; and they are interesting to read." Little more need be said.

A Woman Without Substance: A Character Analysis of Olenka from "The Darling"

In the course of our lives we have all met a woman who has not developed thoughts, feelings or even her own sense of well being. This female always needs to be involved in a relationship which confirms her self worth and identity. She will ask a single, unattached woman how she can stand to be alone. Such a woman is Olenka Semyonovna in Anton Chekhov's "The Darling." This behavior raises the question about how a woman like Olenka functions with others and why anyone would call her "The Darling." An analysis of her character will answer this question.

First of all, Anton Chekhov describes Olenka as very pleasant to look at. She is cherubic in appearance: ". . . full rosy cheeks, her soft white neck with a dark mole on it, and the kind naive smile . . ." (page 156). Her innocent child-like beauty is appealing to men and at the same time non-threatening to women. Had Olenka been an unearthly beauty, other females would have been less comfortable in her presence and less trusting, but as she is simply adorable they have no fear of showing her affection and kindness. Men might well have found her unapproachable had she been overly beautiful.

Olenka's appearance is not the only thing childlike about her. She has the blind, absolute devotion of a child. But while her love is seemingly innocent, it is parasitic. Olenka is an emotional vampire and intellectual leech. From those that she professes to love she drains not only life and liveliness, but also their identities. This semiconscious act affects all of the males she is involved with, her two husbands, a lover and his son.

Olenka's first husband is Ivan Petrovitch, also called Kukin, the manager of a theater not far from her home. Like most actors Kukin is very dramatic. Often he is found raging at the sky for the weather that ruins his productions and the ignorance that afflicts the population's inability to appreciate his craft. Olenka listens to his tirades, serving as an absorbed listener, riveted to his every word. Before long she is infatuated ". . . there was a sweet thrill in her heart, she had no desire to sleep . . ." (page 156).

After a brief courtship, the two are married. And like a sponge she absorbs all of Kukin's ideas and values. She sees the theater as ". . . the most important thing in life . . ." (page 156). When she is with her friends or the actors, she expresses her husband's irritation with the populace for their thoughtless view of art as though it were her own. Throughout their life together physical manifestations of what is psychologically happening within their relationship appear. Olenka becomes more robust with age and good health. Kukin, already sallow to begin with, becomes ". . . thinner and yellower . . ." (page 156) with a chronic illness.

Under his wife's care his vitality does not return and while away on business he dies. Following his demise, Olenka is distraught, cries a great deal and receives the pity and condolences of her neighbors. In spite of her behavior, Kukin's death seems to have touched her only on the surface. Within three months she meets Vassily Andretic Pustovalov, manager of a timber company and quickly recovers from her grief. He will become her second husband.

After one meeting she thinks of him continuously. Later, following a visit from a match maker, Pustovalov pays Olenka a visit. Before his visit, Olenka had simply liked him very much; afterwards she was sure that she loved him. Her infatuation becomes frenzied and thus she "... loved him so much that she lays awake all night in a perfect fever ..." (page 158). This feeling is similar to what she felt for her first husband.

Once Olenka marries Pustovalov, the emotional and physical drainage begins. Olenka leeches from her spouse all of his ideas and worries about the cost of shipping timber and the price the wood must be sold at. She even begins to dream of timber. And as before, she goes to all of her friends and acquaintances spouting expert opinions as though she were the owner of the timber company herself. Soon Pustovalov's health fails. He dies of a fever and she is alone again, but not for long. She is never alone for long. Sometime before the death of her second husband, she meets Smirnin, a soldier trained as a veterinarian. He is separated from his wife and child when he comes to her lodge and would keep her company while Pustovalov was away.

Smirnin is not like any of the other men in Olenka's life. All of the men that preceded him thought nothing of allowing their lives to become hers. But when she tries to talk about his profession, he becomes irritated, pulling her aside and telling her "... do not talk about what you don't know ..." (page 160). She is hurt by his rebuke, not understanding that she is the source of his exasperation. Perhaps Smirnin was able to refuse her because he never married her, or maybe he simply wanted and expected her to be her own person, not a mirror reflecting himself.

The last victim of Olenka's admiration is Smirnin's son, Sasha, who Olenka meets after a period of time on her own. The ten-year-old boy arrives at her lodge with his reconciled parents. Olenka feels that Sasha is being neglected and takes him under her wing. In her home she tries to physically and emotionally smother him while he struggles to grow. She cannot face the thought of Sasha leaving her to rejoin his parents and go to school. Upset and dismayed, she tries to convince the boy that he needs her. Sasha fights her and tells her to go away. He wishes to grow and doesn't desire her constant doting. At the end of the story Sasha says in his sleep "I'll give it to you! Get away! Shut up!" (page 163). I believe he is referring to his own identity and inner vitality which, if he remains in her care any longer, she will take away by her gentle, beguiling force.

Were Olenka not so destructive and consuming, she might merit some measure of pity. Instead she is a pathetic figure who has created her own situation by neither evolving nor maturing at any point in the story. When given the opportunity to be alone before she meets Sasha, she does not even make an effort at personal growth. She would rather fester in her own anguish.

During this period of solitude Olenka's true personality emerges. Or to be honest, her lack of personality emerges. Before she has served as a mirror, reflecting the personality of her men. Now she is an empty vessel revealing that she does not even have the capacity to care.

All she does is fantasize about what she believes is the perfect love, ". . . a love that would absorb her whole being, her whole soul and reason . . ." (page 161). This is why she refuses the affection of her kitten, pushing it and telling it to go away. The animal could give her love but not in the way Olenka wants. The cat has no identity or opinions that she can take as her own.

Her deterioration is both physically and psychologically visible. In body she is no longer energetic and hardy but thin and plain. The people she knew before begin to avoid her. She visits no one and no one visits her as she has nothing to say or offer.

Her home becomes as dilapidated as she is. Her yard is overrun by prickly weeds, a symbol of the bitterness in her being. And the house itself falls into disrepair. With no one to depend on for ideas and opinions she is unable to care for herself or her dwelling. It is ironic that while Olenka sits and rots unable to evolve, the neighborhood and town around her develops and changes.

Knowing all of this, a question remains, how can anyone call her "darling"? The men she has married and cared for call her "darling" because she makes them the center of her universe, the focus of her worship. To others that surround her, she is compliant and credulous. For instance, while she is helping Kukin in the theater and is lied to or cheated by the actors she has given assistance to, she does not complain or confront them. Instead she mourns their indifference to her feelings and lack of care alone. This is the way she is with all persons in her life.

There is really very little good that can be said for Olenka. She is a weak-minded ignorant woman, having never learned to value or enjoy her own company, which is essential to maturity. For someone who has developed her own sense of well being, it is difficult to pity someone like Olenka who simply refuses to evolve or rely on herself instead of others when given the opportunity.

Wedded Bliss and Wandering Eyes

A young couple smiling, laughing, strolling arm-in-arm along Fifth Avenue may seem to be the portrait of marital bliss to those who pass them on the street, but the readers of Irwin Shaw's "The Girls in Their Summer Dresses" are allowed a closer look. Michael Loomis has an uncontrollable habit of admiring passing women, and his loving wife, Frances, can only take so much before her patience wears thin. When the discussion of this topic brings her insecurities to a new peak, she is faced with the reality that her husband's love is not what she believed it was, and readers get a glimpse into the minds of two partners whose ideas about marriage differ considerably. Shaw illustrates Mike and

Frances's attitudes in the way they speak, their body language and, in a few cases, by clarifying the unspoken thoughts that cross their minds. By delving into the complex emotional relationship of this pair, the author makes it clear that a smiling young couple is not necessarily an ideal young couple, as things are not always what they seem to be.

Although the two characters reach a serious conflict in their relationship when Frances discovers just how strong Mike's attraction to other women is, this story does not seem to imply a deeper problem between the two. For Mike, looking at pretty women is only natural and should not interfere with his relationship with his wife. He believes that if it does not detract from his love for Frances, she should not be bothered. After all, he has never had trouble over this unrestrained desire to look, but not touch, despite the fact that Frances has been silently bothered by it all along. Part of the reason Michael is so unable to understand his wife's distress over the issue is the fact that he sees all women, even her, merely as objects of physical beauty, with no regard to their emotional depth. This is most evident after the heated discussion ends, when Frances leaves the table to call the Stevensons, and "Michael watche[s] her walk, thinking, what a pretty girl, what nice legs" (1241). He is not wondering if she will be okay, and he is not thinking about how she will deal with what she has just learned. From afar, she is just like every other beautiful woman on Fifth Avenue; she just happens to be the one he married, and that seems to be the primary reason why he loves her.

Shaw conveys this aspect of Michael's personality in such a way that it is easy to become frustrated with him, yet difficult to hate him. Throughout the entire discussion, he never once makes a move with the sole intention of hurting Frances, and he tells her that she does not have to listen to his confession. Mike would rather she live in blissful ignorance, as she would be spared the pain of knowing his desires, and it would certainly make his life much easier. Of course, his motives are selfish, and his way of giving Frances the truth she demands is insensitive, but readers can see past the harshness to attribute this more to immaturity than to ill intentions. Even Frances knows how immature her husband can be, responding to his excitement over the beautiful women by calling it "a kid's feeling" (1239). However, these are two married adults, and immaturity does not excuse his behavior, nor does it change what has been revealed to Frances and the inevitable impact it will have on their relationship.

Just as important to Mike's character is the way he interacts with women, the result of his childishness and chauvinistic outlook. Like many men, he keeps his emotions out of the way, presenting a cool, smooth image of himself, even to his wife, the person who should know him best. Mike knows her vulnerabilities and uses them to his advantage, offering comfort where he thinks it will soften her anger and telling her what she wants to hear until she refuses to believe it anymore. These gestures would seen sincere, even sweet, if presented at face value, but Shaw offers a greater insight into Mike's reasoning. Just as

Frances begins questioning him about his attraction to other women, Mike senses trouble and immediately makes efforts to smooth it over, "press[ing] her elbow tenderly, knowing what he was doing" (1237). Whenever Frances seems to catch on to her husband's tricks, his smooth front drops to a nervous cover. When she initially calls him on his admiration of the woman with the "country-girl complexion," for example, Mike attempts to dismiss the observation with a laugh. While he aims to say, "It's no big deal, nothing to worry about," with the laugh, he actually says, "Oh no, I've been caught, so let's have as little discussion about this as possible." Frances, however, is too smart to fall for this, and—thanks to Shaw's inclusion of Mike's point of view—so are readers.

Frances actually deserves much more credit than her husband gives her. Certainly a "pretty face," she is utterly devoted to Mike and is generally very sensible. After all, she has dealt with Mike's eye-wandering problem very calmly and never jumped to any conclusions until this particular Sunday—a day that was supposed to be theirs and theirs alone. "I try to make believe it doesn't mean anything," she says. "Some men are just like that, I tell myself, they have to see what they're missing" (1238). Despite her logical approach to her husband's actions, she is smart enough to know that she cannot fool herself forever, and neither can he. This is precisely what leads her to demand the truth about his extramarital interests, as she believes that if he cannot give her the level of commitment she wants, he at least owes her an explanation. She views marriage very differently than Mike does, and this is the main reason why his habits create such a problem between them. While he simply lives *with* her, she lives *for* him, as is apparent in her idea to spend a Sunday together, mainly enjoying activities of his preference. They both agree that she is a good wife, someone who loves him, listens to him and takes care of his household, although Mike seems to think that being a good husband means taking advantage of those things, as he tries to justify his dedication by asking, "Whenever something good happens, don't I run to you? When something bad happens, don't I cry on your shoulder?" (1237). This, along with the fact that he has yet to cheat on her, is what Mike believes makes him a good husband, but Frances takes her commitment much more seriously. To her, Mike's behavior is nothing impressive—it is not even acceptable after five years of marriage.

Shaw's presentation of Frances differs slightly from that of Mike, as readers never get to know what thoughts she is keeping to herself. Her feelings and attitudes are clear, nonetheless, as the author does not have to provide additional information to give the readers a fair impression of Frances for who she really is. Unlike her husband, she does not hide personal information, and she is not concerned with controlling her emotions. From her public display of affection on Fifth Avenue to her straightforward questioning of Mike in the bar, she is clearly in touch with her emotions and is not afraid to show them. Also, this story revolves around Michael's descriptions of feelings and events; Frances merely asks the questions and then reacts to his answers very naturally. She is not asked to reveal anything, therefore readers never really have to wonder if she is telling the truth. Unlike Mike, however, she does not handle situations by avoiding problems to make life as easy as possible; she has a concern, and she is ready to face it head-on. When she finally backs down from her questioning at the end and decides to call the Stevensons, she is not trying to escape a sticky situation by taking the easiest way out. By that point, she had learned everything she ever could have wanted to know about Mike's secret desires, and she knew that nothing productive could come from further discussion of an exhausted topic.

The story's ending brings Mike and Frances right back to where they began, as far as an outside observer would be concerned. They revert back to their plan to visit the Stevensons, just as they had intended to do prior to Frances's grand Sunday plans and the discussion that brought them crashing back down. Despite the fact that the two are once again agreeing to do something together, their personal motives are worlds apart, and they are emotionally in a very different place than they were when the story began. Their opposing feelings about the components of a successful marriage have driven a wedge between the two, and although it might be invisible to the casual outsider, it is undeniable in the eyes of Shaw's readers.

Tobias Wolff's "Powder"

Life is about taking risks. To enjoy existence to the fullest, one must be willing on occasion to step outside the boundaries of custom that society has erected and to venture into the uncharted possibilities of life. This is a part of the over-arching theme in Tobias Wolff's short story "Powder." In this work the reader is presented with two fundamentally different personalities, a father who lives life in the moment, and his obsessively organized son. With extensive use of symbols and figurative language, Wolff develops a deeper understanding of the two conflicting characters and, through the perspective of the narrating son, provides insight into what it means to be alive.

The point of view in "Powder" is first person, told by an older version of the son. The narrator hints at how far removed he is from the story by his reference to himself, "I was a boy" (1350).[1] This suggests a character that has now grown old enough to look back on his past from a more mature perspective. Many of the character developments for the son are less symbolic than those of the father. As the narrator of the story, the son utilizes dialogue to inform the reader about the nature of his past temperament. He muses that he was a boy "who kept his clothes on numbered hangers to ensure proper rotation" (1350), and that he "bothered [his] teachers for homework assignments far ahead of their due dates so that [he] could make up schedules" (1350). This structured behavior is generally considered atypical for a young child who would normally be expected to act in a carefree and playful manner. Perhaps this is the result of growing up in the same home as his incorrigible father, where he was forced to assume the role of responsibility that was otherwise unfulfilled.

The son's unusual adherence to regulation is also indicated through his apprehension during his father's ski trip. The snow had begun to pile up, Christmas dinner was cooking in the oven at home, and the narrator made a point to inform his father of the rashness of continuing. It was to little avail, however, as "he was indifferent to my fretting" (1348). This single sentence serves to illustrate two separate personalities. The reader is given a prudent narrator who knows when to quit, when to pack up and leave lest he miss an important dinner at home. In contrast the reader is given a hint into the easygoing persona of the father. Where the far-sighted son can see the potential troubles of staying out for another run, the father "observed some quality" in the snow "that made it necessary for [them] to get in one last run" (1348). The use of the word "necessary" is interesting and invokes a sense that the father had little choice in the matter. His nature demanded he take advantage of the situation he was given. Further reading of the story only serves to solidify this view.

The narrator makes use of an extensive set of symbols to illustrate the father's often reckless approach to life. It all begins with a barricade that blocks the road out of town. From the son's perspective there is a dark connotation to the word "barricade" that foreshadows the action to come. When the officer states "The road is closed" (1348), there is a sense of finality in its abruptness. For the narrator this is the end. He plays by the rules and is successfully deterred by the barrier. However, he notes that his father "looked at the barricade for a long time. He seemed to be trying to master the idea of it" (1349). There is the implication that in the father's mind the barricade is not necessarily an end, but only a temporary obstacle.

After leaving the barricade in place, the father and son drive to a small diner where the father slips away from the table momentarily to make a phone call. A minute later the police car that was previously guarding the road block speeds past the window, leaving one to assume that the road is no longer being supervised. Once again, Wolff uses a single moment in the narrative to develop the contrast between the two characters. The narrator mentions "I figured he'd called my mother" (1349). This is naive, and it is what the scrupulous son would have done. However, the scene can be interpreted differently by what the reader has already learned about the father from the beginning of the work, that he is a man who lives life less by the books and more by his own desires and needs of the moment.

This is further evidenced when the father decides to return to the now-unguarded road block. He asks the son to move it aside, binding them together as accomplices. The son muses to himself that the "lie of the road behind us had been marked by our own tracks, but there were no tracks ahead of us" (1349). The lack of any visible guidelines caused apprehension for the narrator as he was a child of schedules and rules. There was nothing visible as a guide, nothing on which to make a plan of action. The only option was to set out in exploration which can be dangerous and unpredictable, two things that were antithetical to the son's personality. However, the father was humming a relaxing tune, "Stars Fell on Alabama" (1349). The narrator clearly realizes a key difference between them. His father has a fondness for taking chances, risks are natural, his whole life is a snow covered roadside.

The symbolism of driving is extended to further describe the qualities of each character. At one point in their excursion the father turns to his son, saying "Don't ever try this yourself" (1349), which he justifies by adding "you need, I don't know—a certain instinct" (1349). He implies that it is an instinct that the boy does not have. On the surface he is referring to his abilities as a driver, but the symbol extends to his traits as a person as well. To be able to navigate in such dangerous conditions requires an ability to change directions in an instant. The father lives his life in the moment, never seeing farther into the future than his immediate needs demand. He even had to "fight for the privilege" of taking his son skiing, as his wife was "still angry with him for sneaking [him] into a nightclub" during their last visit (1348). There is the sense that while the father enjoys a life full of risks without compromise, it is an underlying truth that taking great chances can lead to great disasters. It is not a life that is easy to live.

There is a moment in the story where the father comes to understand himself and the dangerous nature of his personality. He says to the son, "I'm a great driver. That's not a virtue, okay? It's just a fact" (1349). In this instance, Wolff allows the two opposing characters to grow individually by gaining a deeper understanding of each other's differing natures. The father praises the son's ability to plan ahead. He comes to understand that living life in the moment can lead to an unfulfilled future. Likewise, a life of strict planning can lead to monotony, and a similar emptiness. What is needed is a blending of the two ideologies, a willingness to bend and change with the times, but also to look cautiously into the future. Though the father does not undergo any dramatic change over the course of the work, his words have a profound effect on the son.

In the end the son finally comprehends the ways of his father. It is an emotional finale, where the two come to a sort of shared insight of each other. The father realizes that his life of chance and impulse has certain unavoidable consequences, that sometimes even when living in the moment he must be able to realize certain boundaries for himself, such as the "orange stakes" that had "been planted at intervals in two parallel lines" (1350) on the snow covered roadside. Unfortunately, understanding does not guarantee change, and the father appears to end the story much like he began it. However, the son takes to heart the lesson he learns that sometimes one has to take a risk in order to fully appreciate life. Organization and planning are his strengths, but he eventually comes to understand that if "you haven't driven fresh powder" (1350), you haven't truly lived.

STUDYING THE SHORT STORY: ADDITIONAL RESOURCES

This section of the *Reader's Guide* introduces additional resources for studying the short story.

Resources for Library Research

It is likely that most of the papers you will be asked to write in introductory courses in fiction will require little or no formal research, though you should be sure to understand your instructor's views on the subject. On the other hand, as a student of literature you need to be aware of those library resources that are useful in learning more about individual authors and stories as well as the literary tradition to which they belong. A selected number of these works are listed below. Most should be fairly easy to locate on the reference shelves, either through careful browsing or through the library catalog. If you have difficulty in locating any of these works, be sure to ask for help at the reference desk. Reference librarians are very familiar with what your library's resources are and are experienced in locating the kind of information you are seeking. Library resources now routinely include electronic databases on CD-Rom and access to information networks and services including the Internet. Since each library handles its electronic services differently, the reference librarian once again should be consulted.

Guides to Literary Research:
Altick, Richard D. *The Art of Literary Research*. New York: Norton, 1993.
_____, and Andrew D. Wright, *Selective Bibliography for the Study of English and American Literature*. 6th ed. New York: Macmillan, 1979.
Baker, Nancy L., and Nancy Huling. *A Research Guide for Undergraduate Students: English and American Literature*. 5th ed. New York: MLA, 2001.
Bateson, Frederick W., and Harrison T. Meserole, eds. *Guide to English and American Literature*. 3rd ed. London: Longman, 1986.
Bracken, James K. *Reference Works in British and American Literature*, Volume I. Englewood, Colo.: Libraries Unlimited, 1990. Volume II (1991).
Ghodes, Clarence, and E. Marovitz Sanford. *Bibliographical Guide to the Study of the Literature of the U.S.A.* 5th ed. Durham: Duke UP, 1984.

Gibaldi, Joseph. *MLA Handbook for Writers of Research Papers*. 6th ed. New York: MLA, 2003.

Harnar, James L. *Literary Research Guide: A Guide to Reference Sources for the Study of Literatures in English and Related Topics*. 4th ed. New York: MLA, 2002.

Kehler, Dorothea. *Problems in Literary Research: A Guide to Selected Reference Works*. 4th ed. Metuchen, N.J.: Scarecrow P, 1996.

Miller, Robert Henry. *Handbook of Literary Research*. Metuchen, N.J.: Scarecrow Press, 1995.

Schweik, Robert C., and Dieter Riesner. *Reference Sources in English and American Literature: An Annotated Bibliography*. New York: Norton, 1977.

Bibliographies:

Annual Bibliography of English Language and Literature. Cambridge, Eng.: Modern Humanities Research Association, 1920–.

MLA International Bibliography of Books and Articles on the Modern Languages and Literature. New York: MLA, 1921–. Available Online, 1963–.

New Cambridge Bibliography of English Literature. Ed. Ian R. Wilson. Vol. 4: 1900–1950. New York: Cambridge UP, 1982.

Year's Work in English Studies. London: Murray, for the English Association, 1921–.

Bibliographies of Short Fiction Criticism:

Aycock, Wendell M. *Twentieth-Century Short Story Explication: New Series*. Hamden, Conn.: Shoe String P, 1991–1992.

Thurston, Jarvis, ed. *Short Fiction Criticism: A Checklist of Interpretations since 1925 of Stories and Novelettes (American British, Continent 1800–1958.)* Denver: Swallow, 1960.

Walker, Warren S. *Twentieth-Century Short Story Explication: Interpretations 1900–1975 of Short Fiction since 1900*. 3rd ed. Hamden, Conn.: Shoe String P, 1977. Supplement 1 (1980), 2 (1984), 3 (1987), 4 (1989), 5 (1991).

———. *Twentieth-Century Short Story Explication: New Series: 1989–1900 With Checklists of Books and Journals Used*. Vol. 1. Hamden, Conn: Shoe String P, 1993.

Weixelmann, Joe, ed. *American Short Fiction Criticism and Scholarship, 1959–1977: A Checklist*. Chicago: Swallow, 1982.

Periodicals Specializing in Short Fiction Criticism:

Studies in the Short Story. Newberry, S.C.: Newberry College, 1963–. Quarterly. Each summer issue contains a bibliography of short story criticism.

Guides to Literary Criticism:

Articles on Twentieth-Century Literature: An Annotated Bibliography. 1954–1970. Ed. David E. Pownall. 7 vols. Millwood, N.Y.: Kraus, 1973–1980.

Contemporary Literary Criticism: Excerpts from Criticism of the Works of Today's Novelists, Poets, Playwrights and Other Creative Writers. Ed. Sharon R. Gunton. Detroit: Gale, 1973-.

Literary Criticism Index. Ed. Alan R. Wiener and Spencer Means. Metuchen, N.J.: Scarecrow P, 1994.

Nineteenth-Century Literary Criticism: Criticism of the Works of Novelists, Poets, Playwrights, Short Story Writers, Philosophers and Other Creative Writers. Ed. Laurie L. Harris. Detroit: Gale, 1981-.

Twentieth-Century Literary Criticism: Excerpts from Criticism of the Works of Novelists, Poets, Playwrights. Short Story Writers, and Other Creative Writers, 1900-1960. Ed. Dedria Bryfonski, et al. Detroit: Gale, 1978-.

Surveys of Literary History/Companions to Literature:

American Women Writers: A Critical Reference Guide from Colonial Times to the Present. Ed. Lina Mainero. 4 vols. New York: Ungar, 1979.

Baugh, Albert C., et al. *A Literary History of England.* 2nd ed. New York: Prentice Hall, 1967.

British Writers. Ed. Ian-Scott Kilvert. 7 vols. New York: Scribner's, 1979.

Cambridge History of American Literature. 9 vols. Ed. Sacvan Bercovitch. Cambridge, Eng.: Cambridge UP, 1994-2005.

Cambridge History of Literacy Criticism. 9 vols. Ed. H. B. Nisbet and Claude Rowson. Cambridge, Eng.: Cambridge UP, 1993-2005.

Columbia Literary History of the United States. Ed. Emory Elliott. New York: Columbia UP, 1988.

The Companion to Southern Literature: Themes, Genres, Places, People, Movements, and Motifs. Ed. Joseph Flora, et al. Baton Rouge: Louisiana State UP, 2002.

The Concise Oxford Companion to African American Literature. Ed. William L. Andrews et al. New York: Oxford UP, 2001.

The Continuum Encyclopedia of American Literature. Ed. Steven Serafin. New York: Continuum Publishing, 2003.

Critical Survey of Short Fiction. Ed. Frank N. Magill. 7 vols. Englewood Cliffs, N.J.: Salem, 1981.

Daitches, David. *A Critical History of English Literature.* 2 vols. New York: Ronald Press, 1960.

Encyclopedia of American Literature. Ed. Carol Berkin et al. New York: Facts on File, 2002.

Encyclopedia of American War Literature. Ed. Philip K. Jason et al. Westport, CT: Greenwood Publishing, 2000.

HarperCollins Reader's Encyclopedia of American Literature. Ed. George Perkins et al. New York: HarperCollins, 2002.

Literary History of the United States. Ed. Robert E. Spiller. 4th ed. New York: Macmillan, 1974.

Magill's Survey of American Literature. Ed. Frank N. Magill. 8 vols. New York: Marshall Cavendish, 1991.

Merriam-Webster's Encyclopedia of Literature (Springfield, Mass.: Merriam-Webster, Inc., 1995.

The Oxford Companion to African-American Literature. Ed. William L. Andres, et al. New York: Oxford UP, 1997.

The Oxford Companion to American Literature. Ed. James D. Hart. 65th ed. New York: Oxford UP, 1995.

The Oxford Companion to Canadian Literature. Ed. Eugene Benson and William Toye. New York: Oxford UP, 1998.

Oxford Companion to Edwardian Fiction, 1900–1914: New Voices in an Age of Uncertainty. Ed. Sandra Kemp et al. New York: Oxford UP, 2002.

The Oxford Companion to English Literature. Ed. Margaret Drabble. New York: Oxford UP, 2003.

Oxford Companion to German Literature. Ed. Mary Garland. New York: Oxford UP, 1997.

The Oxford Companion to Irish Literature. Ed. Robert Welch. New York: Oxford UP, 1996.

Oxford Companion to Italian Literature. Eds. Peter Hainsworth and David Robey. New York: Oxford UP, 2002.

The Oxford Companion to Women's Writing in the United States. Ed. Cathy N. Davidson and Linda Wagner-Martin. New York: Oxford UP, 1995.

Oxford Encyclopedia of American Literature. Ed. Jay Parini. New York: Oxford UP, 2003.

The Oxford History of English Literature. Oxford, Eng.: Oxford UP, 1945–.

Sources of Biographical Information:

American Authors, 1600–1900. Ed. Stanley J. Kunitz and Howard Haycraft. New York: Wilson, 1977.

British Authors of the Nineteenth Century. Ed. Stanley J. Kunitz and Howard Haycraft. New York: Wilson, 1936.

Concise Dictionary of American Literary Biography. 3rd ed. New York: Scribners, 1989.

Contemporary Authors: A Bio-Bibliographical Guide to Current Writers in Fiction, General Nonfiction, Poetry, Journalism, Drama, Motion Pictures, Television, and Other Fields. Detroit: Gale, 1962–.

Contemporary Authors Autobiography Series. Ed. Linda Metzger. Detroit: Gale, 1984–.

Contemporary Authors New Revision Series. Ed. Ann Evory, Detroit: Gale, 1981.

Dictionary of Literary Biography. Ed. Matthew J. Bruccoli. Detroit: Gale, 1978–.

Vol. 74 *American Short-Story Writers Before 1800.* Ed. Bobby Ellen Kimbel and William E. Grant. (1988)

Vol. 78 *American Short-Story Writers, 1880–1910.* Ed. Bobby Ellen Kimbel. (1989)

Vol. 86 *American Short-Story Writers, 1910–1945: First Series.* Ed. Bobby Ellen Kimbel. (1989)

Vol. 102 *American Short-Story Writers, 1910–1945: Second Series.* Ed. Bobby Ellen Kimbel.

Vol. 130 *American Short-Story Writers Since World War II.* Ed. Patrick Meanor. (1993)

European Authors. 1000–1900. Ed. Stanley J. Kunitz and Vineta Colby. New York: Wilson, 1967.

Twentieth-Century Authors. Ed. Stanley J. Kunitz and Howard Haycraft. New York: Wilson, 1942.

Who's Who in Twentieth-Century Literature. Ed. Martin Seymour. New York: Holt, 1976.

World Authors, 1950–1970: A Companion Volume to Twentieth-Century Authors. Ed. John Wakeman. New York: Wilson, 1975. Supplement, 1870–1975 (1980).

Reminder: Whenever you utilize the work of others, whether in print or electronic format, you must be sure both to record the source of your information and to give that source credit through an appropriate citation.

Resources on the Internet

In an age when millions of American use the Internet each day to access information, it is hardly surprising that the Internet should be an increasingly valuable resource for literary study. Its resources include:

- Free and unlimited access to online catalogs at many of the great libraries of the world, including the Harvard University Library and the Library of Congress, allowing basic bibliographic researching from the comfort of one's own study.

- Online and downloadable texts of an increasingly large number of novels and short stories. The latter include many of the texts included in this edition of *Fiction 100.* Carnegie Mellon University has been making electronic texts available since 1990. Other important and easily accessible sources for e-texts are Project Gutenberg (perhaps the largest and best-known); the British Museum; and the Electronic Text Center at the

University of Virginia. The University of Pennsylvania Library offers a useful e-text search tool (Online-Books).

- Websites dedicated to individual authors, including most of those included in *Fiction 100*. These sites offer biographical and bibliographical information, reviews, text, photographs, and lists of criticism.

- Commercial publisher and university press websites. At Prentice Hall's website you will find an online study resource, The Companion Website, dedicated to this text. The address is: www.prenhall.com/pickering. This site is a comprehensive resource that offers an interactive timeline; author biographies and contextual links; online quizzes which include instant scoring and coaching; writing activities that foster critical thinking; essay questions designed to test critical thinking skills; and a dynamic list of dynamic Web links that provides valuable sources of supplemental information.

- The Electronic Demonstration Center maintained in New York by the Modern Language Association (MLA), where, among other things, you can download MLA's style sheet for citing electronic sources.

- Online writing laboratories (OWLS) located at colleges and universities across the nation. While most of these sites understandably restrict their services to their own students, some, like the one at Purdue University, offer downloadable handouts and services to Internet browsers. At Purdue's website you can access some one hundred handouts on writing and writing-related issues, including a handout on the citation of electronic sources using the MLA format.

- Virtual bookstores, where you can search for and buy books (at a discount). These include Amazon, which advertises itself as the "World's Greatest Bookstore," whose browsable catalog is said to contain a million titles. Other features include the "Daily Spotlight" and information on featured books and authors in the news.

- Reference books: encyclopedias, bibliographies, thesauruses, dictionaries, etc.

- The home pages of English departments and individual English instructors. Instructors often make available their resumes, the syllabi of courses they are teaching or have taught, and, sometimes, examples of their students' papers.

The list quite literally goes on and on. Internet sites, to be sure, vary greatly both in usefulness and quality. They also change daily and are subject to the idiosyncrasies of those who establish and maintain them. Websites that are not maintained, like any other information source, quickly become outdated and simply add to the clutter of the Internet. The main point here, however, is that ready or not, the electronic age has collided with the English classroom.

Gaining access to Internet information, as most of you are aware, is fairly easy. Use any of the established search engines (Google, Fast, Yahoo!, Excite, Infoseek, Atlavista, Webcrawler, Lycos, etc.). Becoming comfortable with this form of knowledge and communication is, of course, mandatory in the world in which we live, and what you learn about searching for information electronically for your English class will stand you in good stead in you other courses as well.

Resources on Film

Film is a kind of literature, both in method and technique, and their defining elements are similar in many ways. To begin with, film and fiction are both narrative modes. Both attempt to arrange or order experience by presenting a sequential series of events that involve such common elements as plot, characterization, setting, point of view, theme, tone, imagery, and symbol. Moreover, both treat their subjects in ways that can be characterized as romantic, realistic, or experimental. Viewing, studying, and analyzing the film version of a story or novel with which we are familiar is a good way to come to understand and appreciate both literary and cinematic art. To be sure, there are major differences between the two mediums, but exploring those differences helps us to understand what happens when literature is translated into film as well as the relative strengths and weaknesses of each genre.

A number of excellent film adaptations of stories included in this edition of *Fiction 100* are currently available at local video stores for a nominal rental fee. Viewing them in connection with the courses you are taking (even if you do so on your own) is an enjoyable experience—one that can lead to a deeper, fuller appreciation of the literary text. It can also make you a more knowledgeable and thoughtful consumer of the films that Hollywood provides. As you ponder the experience of reading with the experience of viewing consider the following questions.

Literature/Film: Ten Questions

1. What devices are used by the author and filmmaker to provide narrative structure?
2. How do author and filmmaker go about suggesting time and the passage of time—both actual (clock) time and psychological time?

3. What techniques do the two mediums employ to establish characterization?

4. How does the filmmaker reveal what is taking place in the mind of the protagonist and the minds of the other characters?

5. What is the point of view of the story? Where is the point of view—the eye of the camera—located on the screen? What effect does the location of the camera's eye have upon the other elements in the film?

6. How do the two media go about establishing setting, mood, and tone? What imagery and symbols do each employ?

7. How is theme presented and revealed to reader and viewer?

8. What specific cinematic techniques does the filmmaker employ—e.g., close-up, middle-distance, and long-range shots; sound effects; flashbacks; and lighting?

9. How faithful has the filmmaker been to the original story? What liberties has he or she taken? What has been added, and what has been left out? Why?

10. Which experience (the film or the printed story) do you find more satisfying? Why?

Adaptations of Short Stories in *Fiction 100* Available on Film and Video

The following short stories in the current edition have been adapted for film and video and many of these are available for rent at your local video outlet:

Author	Story
Sherman Alexie	"This Is What It Means to Say Phoenix, Arizona" (adapted as "Smoke Signals")
Ambrose Bierce	"An Occurrence at Owl Creek Bridge"
Willa Cather	"Paul's Case"
Kate Chopin	"The Story of an Hour" (adapted as "The Joy that Kills")
Joseph Conrad	"The Secret Sharer" (adapted as "Face to Face")
Joseph Conrad	"Heart of Darkness"
Stephen Crane	"The Bride Comes to Yellow Sky"
Arthur Conan Doyle	"A Scandal in Bohemia"
William Faulkner	"Barn Burning"

William Faulkner	"A Rose for Emily"
Charlotte Perkins Gilman	"The Yellow Wall-Paper"
Susan Glaspell	"A Jury of Her Peers"
Nikolai Gogol	"The Overcoat" (adapted as "The Cloak")
Bret Harte	"Tennessee's Partner"
Nathanial Hawthorne	"Young Goodman Brown"
Shirley Jackson	"The Lottery"
Henry James	"The Real Thing"
Sarah Orne Jewett	"A White Heron"
James Joyce	"Araby"
James Joyce	"The Dead"
W. P. Kinsella	"Shoeless Joe Jackson Comes to Iowa" (adapted as "Field of Dreams")
D. H. Lawrence	"The Horse Dealer's Daughter"
	"The Rocking-Horse Winner"
Guy de Maupassant	"The Necklace"
Herman Melville	"Bartleby the Scrivener"
Joyce Carol Oates	"Where Are You Going, Where Have You Been?" (adapted as "Smooth Talk")
Edgar Allan Poe	"The Cask of Amontillado"
Edgar Allan Poe	"The Fall of the House of Usher"
John Steinbeck	"The Chrysanthemums"
Leo Tolstoy	"The Death of Ivan Ilych"
Richard Wright	"The Man Who Was Almost a Man" (adapted as "Almos' a Man")

THE HISTORICAL DEVELOPMENT OF THE SHORT STORY

Beginnings

The short story and the novel as independent and self-conscious literary genres trace their beginnings to eighteenth-century England and to a number of identifiable and far-reaching changes taking place within English society itself. During the first decades of the eighteenth century the forces unleashed by capitalism and the rise of commerce and manufacturing had created new and ever-widening pockets of urban, middle-class society, hungry for culture and possessed with just enough money, leisure, and education to pursue and enjoy it. Theirs was a demand, however, that neither drama nor poetry could fully satisfy, for both of these traditional forms required a developed sense of art and culture, which the untutored middle class rarely shared. Moreover, drama and poetry, especially the latter, had become identified in the common mind with the world of court and country, a world of privilege and tradition that these urban dwellers did not know and with which they could not identify. When the opportunity arose, therefore, it was almost inevitable that the sons and daughters of the middle class should turn instead to prose fiction, first to the novel and somewhat later to the short story—two forms of literary art that existed for the most part quite independent of the established literary standards of the day. That this new reading public should in turn come to influence, if not dictate, fiction's choice of subject matter, theme, and point of view followed almost as a matter of course.

The popular literature of any period tends to capture and reflect the dominant social, economic, political, religious, and scientific climate of the age in which it is written. This was particularly true of eighteenth-century England, where the new scientific rationalism of Newton and Locke conspired with an increasingly fluid and open social and economic order, and a more democratic political system, to attach new importance to the ability of the individual Englishman to make his own choices respecting the affairs of everyday life and thus in a measure control his own destiny. As Ian Watt has observed, "For those fully exposed to the new economic order, the effective entity on which social arrangements were now based was no longer the family, nor the church, nor the guild, nor the township, nor the collective unit, but the individual: he alone was primarily responsible for determining his own economic, social, political, and religious roles."[1]

The eighteenth-century novel, by realistically portraying a world with which ordinary readers could at once identify, clearly reflects this growing spirit of individualization and secularization. Beginning in 1719 with the publication of Daniel Defoe's *Robinson Crusoe*, authors like Samuel Richardson, Henry Fielding, Tobias Smollett, and Laurence Sterne brought forth a series of novels explicitly addressed to the needs and interests of the urban, middle-class readership for which they wrote. Writing for the most part in a plain, unembellished style in keeping with the education of their audience, these authors sought to create convincing characters caught up in a series of misadventures whose solutions served to illustrate the fundamental importance of prudent and proper behavior in an increasingly complicated world. Their successes not only called forth hundreds of imitators but in a relatively short period of time secured for the novel a dominance it has yet to relinquish.

The development of the short story, on the other hand, took a somewhat different course. Although recognizable antecedents of what we now call the short story are to be found occasionally in British newspapers and magazines throughout the eighteenth century, it was not the English authors but their nineteenth-century American counterparts who played the leading role in creating and perfecting the short story as a literary form. Until relatively late in the nineteenth century and the appearance of Rudyard Kipling and Thomas Hardy, the best-known Victorian writers of fiction consistently demonstrated a preference for the novel and left the fate of the short story to others, though they were quick enough to capitalize on the immediate financial advantages afforded by serializing their novels for the magazines before publishing them in book form. When they did attempt short stories, the results were often undistinguished and crude. In Charles Dickens's case, for example, his short pieces, with very few exceptions, were little more than sketches or highly impressionistic essays—clever evocations of the mood and atmosphere of London life—as opposed to symmetrical, unified short stories with carefully developed patterns of plot and action.

The strong preference for the novel was attributable in large measure to the literary tradition in which the Victorian novelists worked. Having been raised and educated within the great tradition of the English novel—the tradition that by 1830 had produced not only Fielding, Richardson, and their contemporaries but Jane Austen and Sir Walter Scott as well—it was perhaps only natural that their methods and techniques (not to mention their temperaments) should become those of the novelist. Novels were what their readers and publishers expected and demanded of them, and readers and publishers were then, as now,

[1]Ian Watt, *The Rise of the Novel: Students in Defoe, Richardson, and Fielding* (Berkeley: U California P, 1957) 61.

powerful taskmasters. Part of this preference for the novel was probably also the result of the peculiar vision or outlook that so characterizes Victorian fiction and sets it at once apart from most American fiction of the same period. The Victorian vision was a broad social one, embracing whole sections of life and society, and predominantly interested in delineating character in its relationship to society as a whole. Such a vision seems, in fact, to have been virtually incapable of rendering a mere slice of life. Rather, it had to serve up "the whole plum pudding," and as a result almost necessitated the expansiveness that only the novel, a three-volume novel at that, could provide. Short fiction was not wholly neglected in nineteenth-century England—the ghost story, the humorous-satirical story, and the retold legend did not find their way into such magazines as *Blackwood's*, *Fraser's*, *Bentley's Miscellany*, and Dickens's own *Household Words*—but it was the sprawling, panoramic novel, not the compact and cohesive short story, that comprised the best of Victorian prose fiction.

In America

In America, on the other hand, a different set of conditions prevailed, which tended to move the would-be author in the direction of the short story. As a result, virtually every important nineteenth-century writer of fiction—Washington Irving, Edgar Allan Poe, Nathaniel Hawthorne, Herman Melville, Mark Twain, Kate Chopin, and Henry James among them—either began as a writer of short fiction or produced at least one noteworthy story during his or her lifetime. At the beginning of the century, as American writers set out on the important task of creating a native literary culture independent from England and the "old world," they found themselves confronted by an obstacle unknown to their British contemporaries. While the American copyright law of 1790 adequately protected the works of home authors, the absence of an international agreement on copyright meant that American publishers were free to pirate and reprint foreign novels without the payment of customary royalties. It was not uncommon, in fact, for American publishers to station agents in London whose sole assignment was to rush copies of new British works aboard ship for transit to America so that those books could be reprinted as quickly as possible. The results were predictable where would-be American authors were concerned. Even in a day in which Americans were loudly proclaiming the need for a literature constructed out of native subject matter and set on native soil, there were comparatively few American publishers with the audacity or vision to underwrite an unknown American novelist, however promising, when they had at their disposal, and for free, a wealth of established English talent upon which to draw.

89

The appearance of the popular miscellany known as the "gift book" or "annual" in the 1820s and 1830s, and the appearance of such famous American magazines as the *Knickerbocker*, *Godey's*, and *Graham's* in the 1830s and 1840s, thus provided a badly needed outlet for the young unestablished American writer who aspired to literary greatness. The periodicals paid cash—about five dollars a page in Melville's time—for fiction that could be published complete in a single issue. The compensation was adequate, if not spectacular, and as a result the magazine came to play an increasingly important role in the development of American literature throughout the nineteenth century and, of course, on into the twentieth. While the artistic quality of the vast bulk of nineteenth-century magazine fiction was probably no higher in America than in England, it is quite clear that almost from the very beginning the short story won an acceptance among writers of unmistakable ability that it was long denied in England. The role played by magazines in the development of the American short story was critical. As Eugene Current-Garcia has observed, "Without the magazine for an outlet, it is doubtful whether the short story would have emerged at all in the United States; lacking this outlet, it certainly could not have prospered."[1]

One is also tempted to attribute something of America's inclination toward short fiction, especially in the present century, to the accelerated, swiftly changing, pragmatic quality of American life itself. In the course of settling a continent, solving the vast political and social problems of a new democratic nation, and building and rebuilding a modern industrialized civilization, Americans have always been a people "on the go" who regard reading as rather a luxury. The emphasis in America has been, and is, on getting things done and getting them done quickly; and this preoccupation with speed and efficiency has been carried over to the national taste in literature as well. The chief advantage of the short story is that it can be read quickly—Poe in his famous 1842 review of Hawthorne's *Twice-Told Tales* insisted, in fact, that a short story should occupy no more than an our of the reader's time. The development of the short story in American thus seems, in retrospect, to have been almost inevitable, precisely because in many ways it mirrors the character and personality of the nation itself. The short story is an art form that allows the American to indulge his or her need for literature and then to get on with the pressing business of day-to-day living.

In both America and England the shifting literary and intellectual climate of the nineteenth century inevitably left its mark on the development of both the novel and short story. This development can be seen not only in the changing assumptions of individual authors about the aims and purposes of fiction itself, but in the conscious choice of subject matter and its

---

[1]Eugene Current Garcia, *The American Short Story Before 1850: A Critical History* (Boston: Twayne, 1985) 1.

manner of treatment as well. As the century unfolds one can trace a general movement away from the subjective romanticism and gothicism of Irving, Poe, Hawthorne, and Sir Walter Scott (including their highly idealized rendering of setting and character) toward the more objective treatment of the realist and naturalist with their deliberate concentration on the commonplace and representative issues of daily life. Plots cease being loose, episodic, and melodramatic, and become close-knit and frequently subordinate to such other concerns as character. One notes as well the changing role of the narrator and the increasingly sophisticated use of point of view. The narrator in many cases ceases to be a disembodied authorial voice standing outside the story; instead the narrator moves inside to become immersed and lost in the personality of one or more of the characters. Style changes too. Where once it was discursive, formal, and often highly "literary," style becomes increasingly rooted in the speech patterns of ordinary, everyday men and women. Style itself becomes a means of creating and sustaining the desired verisimilitude.

In France and Russia

In France and Russia, the two other major Western centers of nineteenth-century literary activity, the historical pattern of development—despite obvious national differences—was much the same. In France as in England the appearance and success of the novel can be traced directly to the rapid advances made in the technology of printing and to the values and tastes of a growing middle-class readership. Despite the fact that the realistic novel, with its close and often critical rendering of society, quickly became the dominant mode of nineteenth-century French fiction, the short story was not neglected, thanks to the proliferation of newspapers supported by advertising revenues and the rise of the monthly periodical. The French short story as a self-conscious art form dates from about 1830 (Prosper Merimee published his first short story, "Mateo Falcone," in 1829), the year in which the great French novelists of the century began to make their appearance. Public acceptance came almost immediately, and within the space of a single decade the short story had established itself as a recognized genre to which many of the most gifted writers of the century were willing to turn their talents. Honore de Balzac, Stendhal, Gustave Flaubert, and Emile Zola, the four great novelists of the century, all tried their hands at the short story, and their example was inevitably copied by others. As in America (but not in England) the quality of French nineteenth-century short fiction was high, culminating in the disarming, close-knit tales of Guy de Maupassant as the century drew to a close.

In Imperial Russia the bulky monthly reviews—the so-called "fat journals," headquartered in Moscow and St. Petersburg—provided the major outlet for the country's nineteenth-century fiction. Although a conservative and feudal aristocracy, bureaucratic governmental interference, and political censorship were facts of life in Czarist Russia, the "fat journals," perhaps because they were few in number and select in readership, managed to survive, and by the 1880s at least a dozen reviews could boast a circulation of nine to ten thousand copies per issue. *The Contemporary*, founded by Alexander Pushkin, published most of Ivan Turgenev's influential *Sportsman's Sketches* and serialized his first two novels; *Notes of the Fatherland* (1830-1884) serialized two early novels by Feodor Dostoevsky; *The Russian Herald* (1856-1887) published Dostoevsky's *Crime and Punishment* and *The Brothers Karamazov*, several of Turgenev's novels, and parts of Leo Tolstoy's *War and Peace* and *Anna Karenina;* and *The Russian Idea* (1880-1918) published most of Anton Chekov's better known short stories. The importance of fiction to the cause of cultivating and sustaining independent, progressive thinking within Czarist Russia far transcended its relatively small audience. As Walter Allen notes, with particular reference to authors like Dostoevsky and Turgenev, "since fiction was often the only place in which dangerous thoughts could be discussed, not always with perfect safety to the novelist, the novel became the main vehicle of criticism—of society, of morals, of the Russian attitude to the West, of man's relation to God and to his fellows, indeed of Russian man in relation to the whole world, visible and invisible, in which he lived."[1]

Some of the reasons that the short story should make considerable headway in nineteenth-century America, France, and Russia while languishing, relatively speaking, in England have been explored above. Irish author Frank O'Connor (1903-1966), in his perceptive and challenging short volume *The Lonely Voice* (1963), offers still another possible explanation, perhaps the most intriguing of all. For O'Connor, himself one of the great storytellers of the twentieth century, the emergence of the short story in different countries is to be traced to "a difference in the national attitude toward society." "I am strongly suggesting," O'Connor writes

> that we can see in it [the short story] an attitude of mind that is attracted by submerged population groups, whatever these may be at any given time—tramps, artists, lonely idealists, dreamers, and spoiled priests. The novel can still adhere to the classical concept of civilized society, of man as an animal who lives in a community, as in Jane Austen and Trollope it obviously does; but the short story

[1]Walter Allen, *The English Novel: A Short Critical History* (New York: Dutton, 1954) 155.

remains by its very nature remote from the community–romantic, individualistic, and intransigents.[2]

Such a theory would, of course, account for why the American short story has become "a national art form." America has traditionally been, and in many crucial ways still is, a land of heterogeneous population groupings—"submerged population groups" to use O'Connor's phrase—whose very pluralism and diversity has had a decided impact on its artistic and intellectual development. Although O'Connor unfortunately did not live long enough to develop his theory in any but the most sketchy way, it remains an intriguing hypothesis that merits further elaboration and discussion.

The Short Story in the Twentieth Century and Beyond

By the end of the nineteenth century narrative prose fiction had become firmly established in both Europe and America as the dominant form of literary art, at least as far as most readers and literary consumers were concerned. The recently concluded twentieth century did little to reverse that trend. Although the achievements of twentieth-century drama and poetry were significant, and in many instances profound, the fact remained that for the average reader the easiest, most direct, and most convincing access to the "felt life" of the times was through the short story and the novel. That twentieth-century readers should continue to respond to fiction takes nothing away from the inherent power of either drama or poetry. The fact that they do only confirms what we know to be true: that in variety and quality, as well as in sheer quantity, the accomplishment of fiction in the twentieth century was impressive.

    The development of fiction in the twentieth century can perhaps best be understood in relation to the changing intellectual climate of the century itself—to what man has come to learn about himself, about the world in which he lives, and about the increasingly uncertain connection between the two. Confronted by new scientific discoveries, the maturation of industrial technology, and the disillusionment and widespread economic and social dislocation that followed World War I, many of the old comforting verities and assurances that constituted the Victorian outlook gave way. Discoveries in physics served to cast doubt on many of the long-accepted postulates of science, including the concept of physical reality itself. Discoveries in biology and psychology seemed

---

[2]Frank O'Connor, *The Lonely Voice: A Study of the Short Story* (Cleveland: World, 1963) xiv.

to confirm a deterministic and behavioristic view of human nature, directly challenging older beliefs about the relationship between mind and body; while the work of Sigmund Freud and his student Carl Jung suggested that the key to human behavior lay beneath the surface of character and personality in the hidden recesses of the subconscious.

Such discoveries, taken together, raised among other things serious questions about where reality itself could finally be located; and while it is perfectly true that such ideas never touched the popular mind in any deep or permanent way, their impact in intellectual circles, including literary men and women, was profound. For the twentieth-century writer the lesson was plain enough: the realistic surface of life could not be trusted or taken for granted. To find "reality" and to participate in the real drama of human events one must continually probe beneath the surface in an attempt to capture, if only for a moment, the fleeting reality of things.

The most characteristic and representative twentieth-century fiction fully reflected this impulse to probe and analyze. In terms of literary technique, this impetus was most apparent in the emphasis on plot and character. Older, more traditional authors tended to direct the reader's attention to plot—that is, to a series of events put together in chronological, linear fashion "to tell a good story"—and to present their characters in terms of how they responded or reacted to those events. Modern authors, on the other hand, tend to reverse this emphasis: their interest is less on "what happens *to* character" than "what happens *in* character." That is, the author, from the beginning, focuses the attention of the reader on the characters, and is interested in the events of plot to the extent that a character's emotional, intellectual, or physical response serves to reveal or develop his or her values, personality, or psychological state.

This analysis of character is apparent as well in the subject matter of twentieth-century fiction. Although many modern and contemporary writers turned the attention of their fiction to examining the social and political fabric of twentieth-century life, they characteristically do so in order to illustrate, document, or explore the progress of individuals who are being asked to cope with a world where fixed and permanent values are often suspect or found to be wanting altogether. Such words as "isolation," "aloneness," and "alienation" frequently recur in reference to modern literature in response to a vision of life which, cut off from the certainties of the past, lives in a chronic state of unease and self-examination. At times, particularly in the years following World War II, such a vision of the human predicament encouraged authors to experiment with new and radical literary techniques. Writing against a backdrop of fragmented experience and discontinuity (if not outright unmeaning), such authors as Flannery O'Connor, Donald Barthelme, Joyce Carol Oates, and Gabriel García Márquez set before us a fiction of wild unpredictability, in which action and event (plot) are hard to follow or nonexistent, characters are barely present if at all, and the other traditional narrative techniques and conventions of the realistic story are so transformed or distorted as to confuse and perplex even the most sophisticated readers. Gone is the whole middle range of experience in which most of us live. In its place the reader encounters the bizarre and grotesque, a highly subjective world of fantasy, neurosis, and madness in which nothing is reassuring and familiar and where "reality" is almost incomprehensible. In its most extreme form such experimentation produced the "anti-novel" or "anti-story" in which the author virtually abandons his or her concerns with "subject," "meaning," and "form," as those terms have been traditionally defined. As might be expected, the "success" of such experiments has become the subject of intense critical debate.

Generalizations such as those described above are, of course, inherently dangerous, for they tell only part of the truth about twentieth-century novels and short stories, most of which continued to do, in a fairly traditional manner, what fiction has always done so well: tell an interesting story in an interesting way. It is true as well that here we have been largely discussing "elite" fiction—the kind of fiction that experienced readers and critics predict will have lasting merit—at the expense of popular fiction—the spy and detective story, the western, the gothic romance, science and speculative fiction, and fantasy—which, as any reader knows full well, competes with and indeed dominates the kind of fiction reviewed by the *New York Review of Books* and the *New York Times*. Such a state of affairs is by no means new or unexpected, since popular and elite fiction have existed comfortably side by side, particularly in magazines, since the eighteenth century. Nor is the distinction, which is usually made on the grounds of intrinsic quality or merit, necessarily an invidious one, for many educated readers (and authors) including professors of English enjoy works of both kinds and manage to shift their attention from one to the other without excessive guilt or apparent loss of literary sophistication. The very quantity of today's mass-produced, mass-marketed fiction does, however, pose an additional challenge for any reader who is seriously interested in improving his or her critical ability—the challenge to demonstrate how and why one work is better or more satisfactory than another.

The history of the short story in the twentieth century is an interesting and exciting one. The influence of French and Russian authors was, on the whole, relatively slight, and the credit for the excellence the short story has achieved belongs once again to America and to a lesser but still important extent to Great Britain and Ireland. To be sure, Russia, despite the burdens imposed on the literary artist by Communist ideology, boasted such skillful story writers as Isaac Babel, Maxim Gorky, Boris Pasternak, and Alexander Solzhenitsyn; and twentieth-century France produced Albert Camus, Jean Paul Sartre, Alain Robbe-Grillet, and others. Argentina has Jorge Luis Borges; Columbia, Gabriel García Márquez; Mexico, Juan Rulfo; Spain, Miguel de Unamuno; Germany, Thomas Mann and Franz Kafka; Japan, Yukio Mishima; Canada, Morley Callaghan, Margaret Atwood, and Alice Munro. Still, in numbers and in quality, the advantage in the past century clearly lay with American, British, and Irish authors—with Sherwood Anderson, Kay Boyle, John Cheever, William Faulkner, F. Scott Fitzgerald, Ernest Hemingway, Henry James, James Joyce, Rudyard Kipling, D. H. Lawrence, Doris Lessing, Bernard Malamud, Katherine Mansfield, Flannery O'Connor, Frank O'Connor, Katherine Anne Porter, John Updike, and Eudora Welty, to cite only a few of the writers represented in the current edition of *Fiction 100.*

Although twentieth-century publishers, aided by the "paperback revolution" of the 1950s and 1960s, to some extent managed to overcome the reluctance of their nineteenth-century counterparts to publish volumes of collected stories, the success of short fiction in the past was very much tied to the existence of the periodical. Yet, paradoxically, the last sixty years—which may quite properly be regarded as the high water mark of the short story—has also been a period in which the big-circulation well-paying magazines of the late 1940s and 1950s as *Saturday Evening Post* (which once sold for a nickel), *Collier's, Red Book,* and *This Week,* whose combined audience at one point reportedly reached sixty million readers. To be sure, the stock in trade of such editorially conservative magazines was the "slick" story, facile in situation, plot, and characterization, of a type that could be counted on to please (and certainly not offend) their vast middle-class clientele. Occasionally, however, they published quality stories as well. Stories by William Faulkner, Ernest Hemingway, and F. Scott Fitzgerald, for example, appeared frequently in the *Saturday Evening Post.* (The *Post,* over the years, in fact, published almost seventy stories by Fitzgerald alone.)[1]

The field of large-circulation magazines regularly offering quality stories has today narrowed down to the likes of *The New Yorker, The Atlantic Monthly, Harper's Magazine, Esquire,* and *Playboy,* magazines that are designed to appeal to rather select and specialized audiences. Though the stories carried in *The New Yorker* have sometimes been criticized for the similarity of their subject matter, tone, technique, and audience, its list of authors reads over the years like a literary "Who's Who": Alice Adams, Sherwood Anderson, Donald Barthelme, Jorge Luis Borges, John Cheever, Alice Munro, Isaac Bashevis Singer, James Thurber, and John Updike, to name only a few. William Peden is certainly correct when he observes that "Over the long haul, issue in and issue out, it has published more good fiction than any other magazine in America."[2]

---

[1] Not surprising, as Philip Stevick notes, "there was a price to be paid. Joseph Blotner, in his life of Faulkner, recorded episodes in which Faulkner revised a rejected story, modifying the baroque intricacies of his prose and muting his idiosyncratic voice." Philip Stevick, *The American Short Story, 1900–1945: A Critical History* (Boston: Twayne, 1984) 8.

[2] William Peden, *The American Short Story: Front Line in the National Defense of Literature* (Boston: Houghton Mifflin, 1964) 22.

Much of the burden for publishing short fiction in recent years, has fallen upon the "little magazines," once mainly the refuge of impecunious poets, many of them university-affiliated or sponsored: for example, the *Yale Review*, *TriQuarterly*, *Sewanee Review*, *Chicago Review*, *Georgia Review*, *Iowa Review*, *Kenyon Review*, *Antioch Review*, *Virginia Quarterly Review*, *Paris Review*, *South Atlantic Quarterly*, *Massachusetts Review*, *Colorado Review*, and *Prairie Schooner*. Limited severely by their small advertising revenue; rising printing, production, and mailing costs; small staffs; small circulations; and their inability to pay their authors any but the most modest of honoraria, many of these "little" magazines live continually on the brink of financial disaster. Happily for the contemporary short story, most of the better ones continue to survive. That they are able to do so is attributable in large measure to the willingness of their contributors to forgo immediate financial reward, though of course all authors hope that with sufficient exposure (and the creation of an audience) a trade house will agree to pick up and publish their stories in collected book form. Not surprisingly, many of these authors are themselves academics, making their homes on college and university campuses where they earn their livelihood as writers in residence or professors of English. Of the writers represented in *Fiction 100*, Donald Barthelme, Ann Beattie, Saul Bellow, Kay Boyle, Raymond Carver, William Faulkner, Louise Erdrich, Pam Houston, Bernard Malamud, Joyce Carol Oates, Frank O'Connor, Robert Phillips, Judy Troy, Alice Walker, and Tobias Wolff have at one time or another taken up residence on the college campus.

Although periodically there are doomsayers who predict its decline, the short story continues to flourish, and, for the present at least, the optimists seem to have the better of the argument. For William Peden, the continuing success of short fiction, especially in America, is attributable to its ability to capture and communicate a world in flux: "The short story in America has always been a thing of individuality, freedom, and variety. Flexibility is its hallmark, and no other literary form is so close to the rapidly changing pulse of the time in which it is written and which in turn it reflects with vigor, variety, and verve."[3]

Selected Bibliography

Allen, Walter. *The Short Story in English*. New York: Oxford UP, 1980.
Averill, Deborah. *The Irish Short Story from George Moore to Frank O'Connor*. Washington: UP America, 1982.

---

[3]Ibid., 6.

Baker, A. L. "The Structure of the Modern Short Story." *College English* 7 (November 1945): 86-92.

Baker, Howard. "The Contemporary Short Story." *Southern Review* 3 (1938): 576-596.

Baldeschwiler, Eileen. "The Lyric Short Story: The Sketch of a History." *Studies in Short Fiction* 6 (1969): 443-453.

Baldwin, Dean. "The Tardy Evolution of the British Short Story." *Studies in Short Fiction* 30 (1993): 23-33.

Bates, H. E. *The Modern Short Story: A Critical Survey.* London: Nelson, 1941.

Bayley, John. *The Short Story: Henry James to Elizabeth Bowen.* New York: St. Martin's, 1988.

Beechcroft, Thomas Owen. *The English Short Story.* London: Longman's Green, 1964.

Berces, Francis. "Poe and the Imagination: An Aesthetic for the Short Story Form." *Journal of the Short Story in English* 2 (1984) 105-113.

Benson, Eugene and William Toye, eds. *The Oxford Companion to Canadian Literature.* Toronto: Oxford UP, 1997.

Bone, Robert. *Down Home: A History of Afro-American Short Fiction from Its Beginnings to the End of the Harlem Renaissance.* New York: Columbia UP, 1988.

Bonheim, Helmut. *The Narrative Modes: Techniques of the Short Story.* Cambridge, Eng.: D. S. Brewster, 1982.

Brown, Julie. *American Women Short Story Writers: A Collection of Critical Essays.* New York: Garland, 1995.

_____, ed. *Ethnicity and the American Short Story* (New York: Garland Publishing, 1997).

Bruck, Peter, ed. *The Black American Short Story in the Twentieth Century: A Collection of Critical Essays* (Amsterdam: B. R. Gruner Publishing Co., 1997).

Canby, Henry S. *The Short Story in English.* New York: Holt, Rinehart, and Winston, 1909.

Crant, Philip A., ed. *The French Short Story.* Columbia: U of South Carolina P, 1975.

Current-Garcia, Eugene. *The American Short Story Before 1850.* Boston: Twayne, 1985.

Fallon, Erin, et. Al. eds. *A Reader's Guide to the Short Story in English* (Westport, Conn.: Greenwood Press, 2001).

Finchow, Peter. "The Americanness of the American Short Story." *Journal of the Short Story in English* 10 (1988): 45-66.

Flora, Joseph, ed. *The English Short Story. 1880-1945: A Critical History.* Boston: Twayne, 1985.

Friedman, Norman. "What Makes the Short Story Short?" *Modern Fiction Studies* 4 (1958): 103-117.

Fusco, Richard. *Maupassant and the American Short Story: The Influence of Form at the Turn of the Century.* University Park: Pennsylvania State UP, 1994.

Gadpaille, Michelle. *The Canadian Short Story*. New York: Oxford UP, 1988.

Garrett, George. "American Short Fiction and the Literary Marketplace." *Sewanee Review* 91 (1983): 112-120.

Gelfant, Blanche H., ed. *The Columbian Companion to the Twentieth-Century American Short Story*. New York: Columbia UP, 2001.

George, Albert J. *Short Fiction in France, 1800-1850*. Syracuse: Syracuse UP, 1964.

Gerlach, John. *Toward the End: Closure and Structure in the American Short Story*. University, Ala.: U Alabama P, 1985.

Gullason, Thomas A. "The Short Story: Revision and Renewal." *Studies in Short Fiction* 19 (1982): 221-230.

_____. "What Makes a 'Great' Short Story Great?" *Studies in Short Fiction* 26 (1989): 267-277.

Hanson, Clare. *Short Stories and Short Fictions, 1880-1980*. New York: St. Martin's, 1985.

Harris, Wendell V. *British Short Fiction in the Nineteenth Century*. Detroit: Wayne State UP, 1979.

Head, Dominic. *The Modernist Short Story: A Study of Theory and Practice*. New York: Cambridge UP, 1992.

Hornyby, Nick. "The *New Yorker* Short Story." *Contemporary American Fiction*. New York: St. Martin's, 1992. 7-29.

Kennedy, J. Gerald, ed. *Modern American Short Story Sequences: Composite Fictions and Fictive Communities* (Cambridge, Eng. Cambridge University Press, 1995).

Kilroy, James, ed. *The Irish Short Story: A Critical History*. Boston, Twayne, 1984.

Levy, Andrew. *The Culture and Commerce of the American Short Story*. New York: Cambridge UP, 1993.

Lohafer, Susan. *Coming to Terms with the Short Story*. Baton Rouge: Louisiana State UP, 1985.

_____, and Jo Ellyn Clarey, eds. *Short Story at a Crossroads*. Baton Rouge: Louisiana State UP, 1989.

MaGill, Frank N., ed. *Critical Survey of Short Fiction*. Rev. ed. Pasadena, Ca.: Salem Press, 1993.

May, Charles E. "From Small Beginnings: Why Did Detective Fiction Make Its Debut in the Short Story Format?" *Armchair Detective* 20 (1987): 77-81.

_____, ed. *Short Story Theories*. Columbus: Ohio State UP, 1976.

Nagel, James. *The Contemporary American Short-Story Cycle: The Ethnic Resonance of Genre* (Baton Rouge: Louisana State University Press, 2001).

New, William H. *Dreams of Speech and Violence: The Art of the Short Story in Canada and New Zealand*. Toronto: U Toronto P, 1987.

_____, ed. *Encyclopedia of Literature in Canada*. Toronto: Toronto UP, 2002.

O'Connor, Frank. *The Lonely Voice: A Study of the Short Story*. Cleveland: World Publishing, 1963.

Orel, Harold. *The Victorian Short Story: Development and Triumph of a Literary Genre*. New York: Cambridge UP, 1986.

O'Toole, L. Michael. *Structure, Style and Interpretation in the Russian Short Story.* New Haven: Yale UP, 1982.

Pattee, Fred Lewis. *The Development of the American Short: An Historical Survey.* New York: Harper and Brothers, 1923.

Peden, Margaret Sayers, ed. *The Latin American Short Story: A Critical History.* Boston: Twayne, 1983.

Peden, William. *The American Short Story: Continuity and Change, 1940–1975.* Boston: Houghton Mifflin, 1975.

_____. "The American Short Story During the Twenties." *Studies in Short Fiction* 10 (1973): 367–371.

_____. *The American Short Story: Front Line in the National Defense of Literature.* Boston: Houghton Mifflin, 1964.

Polsgrove, Carol. "They Made It Pay: British Short Fiction Writers, 1820–1840." *Studies in Short Fiction 11* (1974): 417–421.

Rafroidi, Patrick, and Terence Brown, eds. *The Irish Short Story.* Atlantic Highlands, N.J.: Humanities Press, 1979.

Reid, Ian. *The Short Story.* London: Methuen, 1977.

Rohde, Robert D. *Setting in the American Short Story of Local Color, 1865–1900.* The Hague: Mouton, 1975.

Rohrberger, Mary. *Hawthorne and the Modern Short Story.* The Hague: Mouton, 1966.

Ross, Danforth. *The American Short Story.* Minneapolis: U Minnesota P, 1961.

Shaw, Valerie. *The Short Story: A Critical Introduction.* London: Longman, 1983.

Stephens, Michael. *The Dramaturgy of Style: Voice in Short Fiction.* Carbondale, Ill.: Southern Illinois UP, 1986.

Stevick, Phillip, ed. *The American Short Story, 1900–1945: A Critical History.* Boston: Twayne, 1984.

Tallack, Douglas. *The Nineteenth-Century American Short Story: Language, Form and Ideology.* London: Routledge, 1993.

Thomas, Deborah A. *Dickens and the Short Story.* Philadelphia: U Pennsylvania P, 1982.

Vannata, Dennis. *The English Short Story, 1945–1980: A Critical History.* Boston: Twayne, 1985.

Voss, Arthur. *The American Short Story: A Critical Survey.* Norman: U Oklahoma P, 1973.

Weaver, Gordon. *The American Short Story, 1945–1980: A Critical History.* Boston: Twayne, 1983.

Werlock, Abby H. P. *The Facts on File Companion to the American Short Story* (New York: Facts on File, 2000).

Wright, Austin McGiffert. *The American Short Story in the Twenties.* Chicago: U Chicago P, 1961.